Grammar Expert

Series Editors:
Sarah Bideleux
Gill Mackie

 HEINLE
CENGAGE Learning™

Australia • Brazil • Japan • Korea • Mexico • Singapore • Spain • United Kingdom • United States

Grammar Expert 1
Series Editors: Sarah Bideleux, Gill Mackie

Editorial Director: Joe Dougherty
Consulting Editor: James W. Brown
VP, Director of Content Development:
  Anita Raducanu
Senior Acquisitions Editor: Themis Hatzikos
Director of Content Development: Sarah Bideleux
Project Manager: Diane Flanel Piniaris
Contributing Writers: Rachel Finnie,
  Angela Cussons
Director of Global Field Marketing: Ian Martin
Sr. Print Buyer: Marybeth Hennebury
Art Director: Natasa Arsenidou
Illustrator: Ilias Sounas
Cover/Text Designer: Sophia Fourtouni,
  Natasa Arsenidou
Compositor: Vasiliki Christoforides

ISBN-13: 978-960-403-286-0
ISBN-10: 960-403-286-0

Heinle
25 Thomson Place
Boston, Massachusetts 02210
USA

Cengage Learning is a leading provider of customized learning solutions with office locations around the globe, including Singapore, the United Kingdom, Australia, Mexico, Brazil and Japan. Locate your local office at: **international.cengage.com/region**

Cengage Learning products are represented in Canada by Nelson Education, Ltd.

Visit Heinle online at **elt.heinle.com**
Visit our corporate website at **www.cengage.com**

Printed in China
2 3 4 5 6 7 11 10 09 08

Contents

1 Simple Present & Present Continuous

I USUALLY JOG IN THE MORNING, BUT TODAY I'M RUNNING! I'M LATE FOR WORK AGAIN.

Simple Present

Affirmative	Negative	Question
I work	I do not (don't) work	Do I work?
you work	you do not (don't) work	Do you work?
he works	he does not (doesn't) work	Does he work?
she works	she does not (doesn't) work	Does she work?
it works	it does not (doesn't) work	Does it work?
we work	we do not (don't) work	Do we work?
you work	you do not (don't) work	Do you work?
they work	they do not (don't) work	Do they work?

Short Answers

Yes, I/you do.   No, I/you don't.
Yes, he/she/it does.   No, he/she/it doesn't.
Yes, we/you/they do.   No, we/you/they don't.

We use the Simple Present to talk about:

➤ habits.
   He often goes to the movies.
   I walk in the park every day.

➤ general truths.
   Water boils at 212° F (100° C).
   We make oil from olives.

➤ permanent situations in the present.
   They live in Boston.
   She teaches history and geography.

---

1 ▶ Complete the sentences with the Simple Present.

Ex. *He ....wears........ jeans and T-shirts at home. (wear)*

1   They .... their uncle in Maine every summer. (visit)

2   He .... to the beach for fun. (go)

3   It .... a lot in April. (rain)

4   My friend .... in Washington, D.C. (live)

5   I .... eggs for breakfast. (not eat)

6   Plants .... without water. (die)

7   Mr. Brown .... in an office. (not work)

8   Sally .... for three hours every evening. (study)

9   She .... the piano. (not play)

10 John .... English and French. (speak)

Thinkaboutit

Remember to add **-s** or **-es** to verbs with **he, she** and **it**.

Remember to use **does not/doesn't** for negatives with **he, she** and **it**.

Remember to use **does** for questions with **he, she** and **it**.

2 ► Complete the questions with **do** or **does**.

Ex. ......Does...... he know where the library is?

1 .... they take a vacation in the summer?

2 .... he draw well?

3 .... you usually cook dinner?

4 .... your best friend live near you?

5 .... John have music lessons?

6 .... Angela help you with your work?

7 .... she send e-mails to her friends every day?

8 .... the sun rise in the east?

3 ► Write questions.

Ex. _Do you speak French?_
....
No, I don't speak French.

1 ....
Yes, he lives in the city.

2 ....
No, I don't go to work by bus.

3 ....
Yes, she gets up early on Mondays.

4 ....
Yes, they have lunch at 1 o'clock.

5 ....
No, John doesn't drive a car.

Present Continuous

Affirmative	Negative	Question
I am (I'm) working	I am not (I'm not) working	Am I working?
you are (you're) working	you are not (aren't) working	Are you working?
he is (he's) working	he is not (isn't) working	Is he working?
she is (she's) working	she is not (isn't) working	Is she working?
it is (it's) working	it is not (isn't) working	Is it working?
we are (we're) working	we are not (aren't) working	Are we working?
you are (you're) working	you are not (aren't) working	Are you working?
they are (they're) working	they are not (aren't) working	Are they working?

Short Answers

Yes, I am.	No, I'm not.
Yes, you are.	No, you aren't.
Yes, he/she/it is.	No, he/she/it isn't.
Yes, we/you/they are.	No, we/you/they aren't.

We use the Present Continuous to talk about:

► things that are happening at the time of speaking.
  She is watching TV now.
  I am reading a book.

► things that are happening, but not necessarily at the exact time we are speaking.
  We're studying Italian this year.
  She's working this summer.

Notes

Two contractions of *be* are possible for negative forms with *you, he, she, it, we* and *they*.
You aren't working.   You're not working.
He isn't working.   He's not working.

The negative form with *I* has only one contraction.
I'm not working.

4 ► Complete the sentences with **am**, **are** or **is**.

Ex. The cat ......is...... sleeping.

1 Jane .... driving here.

2 .... you writing a letter?

3 I .... not working in the hotel this summer.

4 My friends .... watching a movie on TV.

5 He .... cleaning his room.

6 They .... playing basketball.

7 We .... waiting for our friends.

8 She .... not listening to the radio.

1

5 ▸ **Write questions.**

Ex. *She is eating an apple.*
    Is she eating an apple?

1 You are making a cake for me.
    ....

2 They are wearing nice clothes.
    ....

3 He is cooking lunch for the family.
    ....

4 The children are swimming in the lake.
    ....

5 She is watering the flowers.
    ....

6 We are driving to the beach.
    ....

6 ▸ **Write the sentences using the short form of the verbs.**

Ex. *I am not eating lunch at home today.*
    I'm not eating lunch at home today.

1 We are not drinking coffee.
    ....

2 They are not listening to the teacher.
    ....

3 I am not learning Chinese.
    ....

4 David is not reading a magazine.
    ....

5 He is not washing his car.
    ....

6 I am not wearing your shirt.
    ....

7 ▸ **Complete the sentences with the Present Continuous.**

Ex. I ......*am studying*...... for finals this month. (study)

1 The neighbors .... a new house. (build)

2 It's Saturday. We .... today. (not work)

3 .... the baby ....? (sleep)

4 We .... the bedroom green. (not paint)

5 I .... you from Washington, D.C. (write)

6 It's Tom's birthday. He .... a party. (have)

Adverbs of Frequency with the Simple Present

never   rarely   sometimes   often/usually   always
0% ◀━━━━━━━━━━━━━━━━━━━━━━━━━━━━━━━━━━━━━━━▶ 100%

Adverbs of frequency come before the main verb but after the verb *to be*.
I never go to concerts.
My brother is often tired at the end of the day.

8 ▸ **Rewrite the sentences with the adverbs of frequency in the correct place.**

Ex. *She goes shopping on Fridays. (always)*
    She always goes shopping on Fridays.

1 He is at home on Sundays. (rarely)
    ....

2 I buy my mother flowers for her birthday. (usually)
    ....

3 Bob reads the newspaper in the morning. (never)
    ....

4 I am late for work. (always)
    ....

5 Does she get home late on Fridays? (often)
    ....

6 Joseph plays the piano at concerts. (sometimes)

Time Expressions with the Simple Present

every day	in the morning
every week	in the afternoon
every month	in the evening
every year	three times a day
every summer	once a week
on Mondays	twice a month
in June	three times a year

Do you work in the evening?
She doesn't wash the dishes every day.

Time Expressions with the Present Continuous

today	this afternoon
at the moment	this week
now	this month
right now	this year
this morning	

I am washing the car at the moment.
Helen and Jack are staying with us this week.

---

9 Complete the chart with the time expressions in the box.

always	at the moment	every week	now	often	on Saturdays
rarely	right now	this evening	this year	today	twice a month

Simple Present	Present Continuous
always	*at the moment*

---

10 Complete the sentences with the Simple Present or Present Continuous.

Ex. *They ....*use*............ their computers every day. (use)*
     *She ....*is flying*............ to Houston today. (fly)*

1 The teacher .... the students about the test at the moment. (tell)

2 .... he .... to his CDs every evening? (listen)

3 I .... a project about fashion this week. (do)

4 She .... in Florida. (not live)

5 .... you .... television right now? (watch)

6 They .... breakfast at the moment. (not have)

7 Fran .... to the office once a week. (come)

8 Jenny rarely .... to the theater. (go)

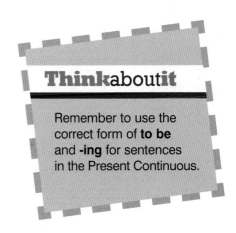

Thinkabout**it**

Remember to use the correct form of **to be** and **-ing** for sentences in the Present Continuous.

Stative Verbs

Stative verbs express states, not actions. We do not usually use these with the Present Continuous. Some common stative verbs are:

➤ verbs of sense:
feel, hear, see, smell, sound, taste.
I see a lot of children in the park.
The soup smells wonderful.

➤ verbs of emotion:
dislike, hate, like, love, need, prefer, want.
They love swimming in the sea.
The dog needs a long walk.

➤ verbs of understanding and opinion:
appear, believe, forget, hope, imagine, know, mean, remember, seem, think, understand.
What do you mean?
She doesn't remember his name.

➤ verbs of possession:
belong, own.
This suitcase belongs to my mother.
I own a red sports car.

---

11 ▶ **Choose the correct answer.**

Ex. He (knows) / is knowing *all the answers to the questions.*

1 This book *belongs / is belonging* to me.

2 Jane *writes / is writing* a letter at the moment.

3 Yes, I *see / am seeing* him.

4 She is playing the piano. It *is sounding / sounds* nice.

5 *Do you believe / Are you believing* in ghosts?

6 They *are washing / wash* the car today.

7 The children *eat / are eating* their lunch now.

8 *I understand / I am understanding* a little Spanish.

12 ▶ **Complete the sentences with the Simple Present or Present Continuous.**

Ex. *My husband ......is riding...... his bicycle today. (ride)*

1 We all .... to a restaurant on Saturday evenings. (go)

2 .... you .... Jane with her work? (help)

3 Sarah .... the violin very well. (not play)

4 .... you usually .... ice cream in the summer? (make)

5 .... she .... the laundry every Saturday? (do)

6 Look! The dog .... the cat! (chase)

7 They always .... fruit in the morning. (eat)

8 I .... you can come to the party with me. (hope)

13 ▶ **Find the mistakes and write the sentences correctly.**

Ex. *Those people are disliking their jobs.*
Those people dislike their jobs.
....

1 I am usually having dinner at 8 o'clock.
....

2 His sister work in a hospital.
....

3 Does he likes basketball?
....

4 What do your brother doing at the moment?
....

5 I starting work at 9 o'clock every morning.
....

6 I am knowing him very well.
....

14 ▶ Choose the correct answer.

Ex. *Greg .... in his office at the moment.*
  a *works* ⓑ *is working*

1 I .... wash my hair every day.
  a right now **b** usually

2 .... Jane speaking to her sister on the phone?
  a Is **b** Does

3 We .... to the park on Sundays.
  a are always going **b** always go

4 He is listening to his favorite CD ....
  a sometimes **b** now

5 This is a wonderful party. I .... a great time!
  a have **b** am having

6 My friends .... the newspaper every day.
  a aren't reading **b** don't read

15 ▶ Write the words in the correct order.

Ex. *in / I / go / swimming / August / often*
  I often go swimming in August.

1 clean / I / on / my / always / room / Sundays
  ....

2 night / often / we / on / pizza / Saturday / eat
  ....

3 your / classical music / does / to / wife / listen / ?
  ....

4 watching / you / this / are / program / ?
  ....

5 tired / evenings / is / Friday / she / on / usually
  ....

6 now / work / you / going / are / to / right / ?
  ....

Pairwork

Work with a partner. Tell your partner two things you do every day, two things you sometimes do and two things you never do.

Writing

Complete the sentences in your own words.

1 I often ....
2 My family never ....
3 At the moment my friend ....
4 On Saturdays I ....
5 Every evening I ....
6 Today ....
7 I sometimes ....
8 In the summer ....

Simple Past & Used To

YOU STARTED THAT REPORT A MONTH AGO! YOU USED TO WORK FASTER BECAUSE YOU DIDN'T USE TO TAKE SO MANY COFFEE BREAKS!

Simple Past – Regular Verbs

Affirmative	Negative	Question
I finished	I did not (didn't) finish	Did I finish?
you finished	you did not (didn't) finish	Did you finish?
he finished	he did not (didn't) finish	Did he finish?
she finished	she did not (didn't) finish	Did she finish?
it finished	it did not (didn't) finish	Did it finish?
we finished	we did not (didn't) finish	Did we finish?
you finished	you did not (didn't) finish	Did you finish?
they finished	they did not (didn't) finish	Did they finish?

Short Answers

Yes, I/you did.	No, I/you didn't.
Yes, he/she/it did.	No, he/she/it didn't.
Yes, we/you/they did.	No, we/you/they didn't.

Simple Past – Irregular Verbs

Affirmative	Negative	Question
I ate	I did not (didn't) eat	Did I eat?
you ate	you did not (didn't) eat	Did you eat?
he ate	he did not (didn't) eat	Did he eat?
she ate	she did not (didn't) eat	Did she eat?
it ate	it did not (didn't) eat	Did it eat?
we ate	we did not (didn't) eat	Did we eat?
you ate	you did not (didn't) eat	Did you eat?
they ate	they did not (didn't) eat	Did they eat?

Short Answers

Yes, I/you did.	No, I/you didn't.
Yes, he/she/it did.	No, he/she/it didn't.
Yes, we/you/they did.	No, we/you/it didn't

We use the Simple Past to talk about:

➤ things that started and finished in the past.
He visited his aunt yesterday.
I lived in Dallas in 2005.

➤ things that happened one after the other in the past.
We parked the car, got our suitcases and went into the airport.
He got dressed, went downstairs and ate breakfast.

➤ things that happened often or were habits in the past.
They played hockey for 12 years.
My son rode his bicycle to school every day.

Notes

We pronounce the -ed in the Simple Past in three different ways.

-id	➔	*wanted*
-t	➔	*watched*
-d	➔	*opened*

See the Irregular Verbs list on page 132.

1 ▶ **Make the sentences negative.**

Ex. *I thought math was easy.*
   I didn't think math was easy.

1 George knew how to get to the train station.
   ....

2 Linda bought bread at the bakery.
   ....

3 The young boy played chess well.
   ....

4 I ate three apples.
   ....

5 Sarah wrote a letter to me.
   ....

2 ▶ **Write questions.**

Ex. *Where* *did you go?* ....
   I went to the beach.

1 When ....
   She left yesterday.

2 Who ....
   I met Jenny.

3 Where ....
   We saw them at the party.

4 What ....
   I said I was sorry.

5 Who ....
   They told their parents.

6 How long ....
   I studied three hours every day.

3 ▶ **Write sentences.**

Ex. *Tom drove to France. (fly)*
   He didn't drive to France. He flew to France

1 My father wrote a book about computers. (read)
   ....

2 Carla sold a new pair of jeans. (buy)
   ....

3 The baseball players lost all their games. (win)
   ....

4 The children walked to the park. (run)
   ....

5 Ed and I drove to work. (take the bus)
   ....

6 Ann and Eva heard a dog in the garden. (see)
   ....

4 ▶ **Complete the text with the Simple Past.**

Last week I (Ex.) ....*saw*........ (see) a fantastic movie. It (1) .... (be) about how people (2) .... (live) thousands of years ago. I (3) .... (know) some of the things they (4) .... (talk) about in the movie but I (5) .... (not know) that life was so difficult. The men (6) .... (hunt) for food and the women (7) .... (do) lots of work, too. They (8) .... (cook) the food and they (9) .... (make) clothes from animal skins. I'm glad I (10) .... (not / be) alive then!

Time Expressions with the Simple Past

yesterday	a week ago
the day before yesterday	a month ago
last night	a year ago
last week	in December
last summer	in 1988
last year	on Sunday
when I was fifteen years old	on June 30th

Time expressions usually come at the beginning or the end of a sentence.
She went to the movies yesterday.
Last year I went on a tour of Australia.

5a ▸ Circle the words and expressions that go with the Simple Past.

an hour ago   in January   in 1998   last Saturday   next week

now   soon   tomorrow   when I'm older   years ago   yesterday

5b ▸ Now write sentences using the Simple Past and the words or expressions from 5a.

Ex.   *I arrived at work an hour ago.* ....

1   ....

2   ....

3   ....

4   ....

5   ....

6 ▸ Write sentences using the Simple Past.

Ex.   *in the sea / swim / last August / I*
       I swam in the sea last August. ....

1   buy / a week ago / we / a lot of furniture

     ....

2   break / the day before yesterday / her glasses / Sally

     ....

3   have / last week / you / a great party

     ....

4   Jane / to her friend / on Monday / an e-mail / send

     ....

5   be / last summer / very hot / it

     ....

6   some good music / hear / yesterday evening / on the radio / I

     ....

7 ▷ **Complete the sentences with the Simple Past.**

Ex.   I .... *sent* .... *a letter to my friend in Japan yesterday. (send)*

1   We .... TV until midnight. (watch)

2   .... he .... his dog? (find)

3   I .... at 7 o'clock on Sunday. (not wake up)

4   She .... to get into the concert. (not pay)

5   They .... a fantastic movie last week. (see)

6   What .... she .... to the party? (wear)

7   The program .... at 11 o'clock. (end)

8   I .... about the accident from my neighbor. (hear)

9   .... they .... to Costa Rica last summer? (fly)

10   She .... shopping this morning. (not go)

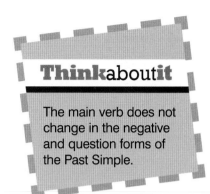

Thinkaboutit

The main verb does not change in the negative and question forms of the Past Simple.

Used To

Affirmative	Negative	Question
I used to play	I did not (didn't) use to play	Did I use to play?
you used to play	you did not (didn't) use to play	Did you use to play?
he used to play	he did not (didn't) use to play	Did he use to play?
she used to play	she did not (didn't) use to play	Did she use to play?
it used to play	it did not (didn't) use to play	Did it use to play?
we used to play	we did not (didn't) use to play	Did we use to play?
you used to play	you did not (didn't) use to play	Did you use to play?
they used to play	they did not (didn't) use to play	Did they use to play?

Short Answers

Yes, I/you did.	No, I/you didn't.
Yes, he/she/it did.	No, he/she/it didn't.
Yes, we/you/they did.	No, we/you/they didn't.

We use *used to* to talk about:

➤ actions that happened often in the past but that don't happen now.
I used to play video games but now I don't.
She didn't use to drive to work, but now she does.

➤ states that existed in the past but that don't exist now.
She used to love skiing but now she prefers snowboarding.

Notes

In negatives and questions, we use *use to*, not *used to*.
He didn't use to study so hard.
Did you use to live in Boston?

8 ▷ **Complete the sentences with used to or use to.**

Ex.   She didn't ...... *use to* ...... understand all the grammar rules but now she does.

1   Did you .... have brown hair?

2   I .... eat two bananas every day. Now I eat two apples.

3   They didn't .... live in New York, but now they do.

4   My daughter .... help me with the housework. Now she has a full-time job.

5   Did you .... watch cartoons on TV?

6   Gordon didn't .... believe in aliens but he does now.

9 ▶ **Write questions.**

Ex. *They used to eat a lot of meat.*
     Did they use to eat a lot of meat?

1 You used to own ten pairs of shoes.

   ....

2 Frank used to cook lunch on Sundays.

   ....

3 I used to live in a big city.

   ....

4 They used to play baseball on Wednesdays.

   ....

5 She used to write a lot of letters.

   ....

6 Simon used to go skiing in Colorado.

   ....

10 ▶ **Complete the sentences with the correct form of used to and the verb in parentheses.**

Ex. *My children ....used to play............ with wooden toys. (play)*

1 I .... milk but now I prefer coffee. (drink)

2 Millions of years ago dinosaurs .... on Earth. (live)

3 Helen .... eggs but now she does. (not like)

4 .... you .... stamps when you were young? (collect)

5 He .... a suit to work but now he doesn't. (wear)

6 Most movies .... in black and white but now they are in color. (be)

7 We .... e-mails but now we do. (not send)

8 .... the world .... colder millions of years ago? (be)

11 ▶ **Complete the sentences in your own words.**

Ex. *Jonathan is very tall but he used to be short.*
     Now I have blond hair but I didn't use to have blond hair.

1 Now people eat pizza and ice cream but ....

   ....

2 I send e-mails to my friends but ....

   ....

3 She wears jeans and T-shirts now but ....

   ....

4 You don't like going to the park but ....

   ....

5 We watch a lot of TV now but ....

   ....

6 He has lots of money now but ....

   ....

Thinkabout**it**

We use the base form of
the verb after **used to**.

12 ▶ **Choose the correct answer.**

Ex. *The children .... games all day yesterday.*
    (a) *played*   **b** *used to play*   **c** *used to*

1   We .... every room in the house last weekend.
     a used to clean   **b** clean   **c** cleaned

2   My friend .... me a mystery novel for my birthday.
     a gave   **b** used to give   **c** given

3   Did you .... live in Chicago?
     a used to   **b** use   **c** use to

4   .... they know the library was closed yesterday?
     a Use   **b** Did they use   **c** Did

5   My son .... work at a university.
     a use to   **b** didn't used   **c** used to

6   I .... the laundry early this morning.
     a used to   **b** did   **c** do

7   .... she use to shop at the department store?
     a Did   **b** Was   **c** Used

8   Thousands of years ago people .... in caves.
     a used to live   **b** used to   **c** live

13 ▶ **Find the mistakes and write the sentences correctly.**

Ex. *We use to live on a farm.*
     We used to live on a farm. ....

     I losed my dog yesterday.
     I lost my dog yesterday. ....

1   Dinosaurs live millions of years ago.
     ....

2   Did you saw the documentary about kangaroos last night?
     ....

3   What did you used to eat when you were a child?
     ....

4   Do you eat your dinner at 8 o'clock yesterday?
     ....

5   What did you did last summer?
     ....

6   I use to enjoy watching basketball on TV.
     ....

7   She didn't knew anyone at my birthday party.
     ....

8   What time he came to work this morning?
     ....

14 ▶ **Match.**

Ex. *We used to*

1   They played

2   Did you live

3   Did people use

4   What time did you

5   I didn't live

6   He didn't use

a   to hunt for food?

b   to like football.

c   *live in an apartment.*

d   chess for two hours last night.

e   in Chicago when I was a child.

f   get up last Sunday?

g   in Texas when you were younger?

Pairwork

Work with a partner. Tell your partner three things you did yesterday.
Tell your partner three things you used to do but you don't do now.

Writing

1   Write a short paragraph about what you
    did last weekend.

....

....

....

....

....

....

....

....

....

....

....

....

....

....

2   Write a short paragraph about what you
    used to do when you were a child.

....

....

....

....

....

....

....

....

....

....

....

....

....

....

I WAS FIXING THE PRINTER. THEN IT GRABBED MY TIE.

Past Continuous

Affirmative	Negative	Question
I was sleeping	I was not (wasn't) sleeping	Was I sleeping?
you were sleeping	you were not (weren't) sleeping	Were you sleeping?
he was sleeping	he was not (wasn't) sleeping	Was he sleeping?
she was sleeping	she was not (wasn't) sleeping	Was she sleeping?
it was sleeping	it was not (wasn't) sleeping	Was it sleeping?
we were sleeping	we were not (weren't) sleeping	Were we sleeping?
you were sleeping	you were not (weren't) sleeping	Were you sleeping?
they were sleeping	they were not (weren't) sleeping	Were they sleeping?

Short Answers

Yes, I was.	No, I wasn't.
Yes, you were.	No, you weren't.
Yes, he/she/it was.	No, he/she/it wasn't.
Yes, we/you/they were.	No, we/you/they weren't.

We use the Past Continuous:

➤ to talk about actions that were in progress at a particular time in the past.
I was writing a letter at 5 o'clock yesterday afternoon.
They were working in Japan last year.

➤ to talk about two or more actions that were in progress at the same time in the past.
He was washing the car and listening to the radio.
At 12 o'clock I was making lunch while John was gardening.

➤ to set the scene of a story.
The sun was shining and the birds were singing in the trees.
The wind was blowing and the baby was crying.

1 ▸ Make the sentences negative.

Ex. *Kevin was working when his wife came home.*
Kevin wasn't working when his wife came home.

1 They were waiting for Martin outside the library.
....

2 I was thinking about my friends.
....

3 The dog was looking for its bone.
....

4 We were walking for a long time.
....

5 Sophie was working on her computer at 7 o'clock.
....

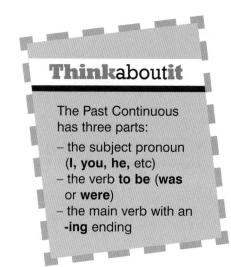

Thinkabout**it**

The Past Continuous has three parts:
– the subject pronoun (**I, you, he,** etc)
– the verb **to be** (**was** or **were**)
– the main verb with an **-ing** ending

2 ▸ Write questions.

Ex. *Those men were drinking orange juice and talking.*
Were those men drinking orange juice and talking?

1 He was looking for the dog in the house.
....

2 They were waiting outside the office for an hour.
....

3 You were learning Spanish last year.
....

4 Leon was talking to Lisa during the English lesson.
....

5 It was snowing yesterday.
....

3 ▸ Complete the sentences with the Past Continuous.

Ex. *He ....was watching........ TV at 9 o'clock last night. (watch)*

1 The dog .... and I .... to sleep. (bark, try)
2 The musicians .... for the concert all week. (practice)
3 She .... in the lake yesterday afternoon. (swim)
4 Who .... the car: you or your father? (drive)
5 I .... very hard all evening. (work)
6 Jake and Lee .... TV while Brian .... the dishes. (watch, wash)
7 The sky was dark and the wind .... (blow)
8 John .... all day yesterday. (study)

Past Continuous and Simple Past

We use the Past Continuous and the Simple Past together when:

➤ one action in the past interrupts another action in the past.
I was sleeping when the phone rang.
They were eating lunch when we arrived.

➤ we tell a story in the past.
We were watching TV when we heard a loud noise outside.
We opened the door and a man was standing there. He was wearing a tall black hat and a coat.

4 **Complete the sentences with the Past Continuous or Simple Past.**

Ex. They ....*were making*.......... breakfast when the doorbell ....*rang*............... . *(make, rang)*

1 The sun .... and the birds .... when I ....
this morning. (shine, sing, wake up)

2 What .... you .... when I .... you? (do, call)

3 I .... a pizza when my grandson .... home. (make, come)

4 When I .... to town, it .... (go, rain)

5 He .... too fast when the accident .... (drive, happen)

6 While I .... home, it .... to rain. (walk, start)

5 **Write questions.**

Ex. what / you watch / on TV / at 8 o'clock last night / ?
What were you watching on TV at 8 o'clock last night? ....

who / she talk to / on the phone / when / I arrive / ?
Who was she talking to on the phone when I arrived? ....

1 where / you play tennis / yesterday afternoon / ?

....

2 what / your friend listen to / while / she cook / ?

....

3 who / you dance with / at the party / last Saturday / ?

....

4 what / the dogs do / when / Brian come home / ?

....

5 what / the teacher say / when / the student arrive / ?

....

6 what / your friends wear / when / you see them / ?

....

6 **Complete the sentences with the Simple Past or Past Continuous.**

Ex. What ....*were you reading*...... in the library when the bell ....*rang*...............? *(you read, ring)*

1 While he .... along the road, a dog .... in front of his car. (drive, run)

2 They .... in Colorado when Mike .... his leg. (ski, break)

3 I .... the car when my friend .... me. (wash, call)

4 While the clothes .... on the line, the wind .... (dry, blow)

5 .... a shower when I .... you? (you take, call)

6 While I .... on the computer, Dan .... a letter. (work, write)

7 Complete the sentences in your own words.

Ex. *When I woke up this morning,* ...the sun was shining....

1 While I was going home, ...

2 When I finished my lunch, ...

3 The cook shouted when ....

4 It was raining while ....

5 What were you doing when ....

6 While Philip was ironing his shirt, ...

7 Jane was watching TV when ....

8 Marty was jogging in the park while ....

8 Choose the correct answer.

Ex. *I* (was dreaming) / *dreamed when the alarm clock* was waking / (woke) *me up.*

1 He *was listening / listened* to music when the CD player *was breaking / broke*.

2 I *was sitting / sat* in the yard when the rain *was starting / started*.

3 What *were you doing / did you* do when the storm *was beginning / began*?

4 The boys *played / were playing* football when Gregory *had / was having* his accident.

5 My husband *cooked / was cooking* in the kitchen when our son *was getting / got* home.

6 When my favorite show *started / was starting* on TV, I *washed / was washing* the dishes.

7 The girls *were eating / ate* spaghetti when Billy *was taking / took* their photograph.

8 When the lights *went / were going* out, we *were thinking / thought* it was an earthquake.

9 Find the mistakes and write the sentences correctly.

Ex. *What were you doing while I saw you in the park yesterday?*
   What were you doing when I saw you in the park yesterday?

1 While I was picking flowers, I suddenly was hearing a loud noise.
   ....

2 Sally was practicing the violin while I reading the newspaper.
   ....

3 They were building a sandcastle when a big wave washing it away.
   ....

4 I sent an e-mail to my best friend when the computer crashed.
   ....

5 The wind was blowing hard when the trees were falling down.
   ....

6 Who did you play chess with when I called you?
   ....

Thinkabout**it**

Always think about which of the two actions took a long time and which happened quickly. Use the Past Continuous for the longer action and the Simple Past for the short action.

10 ▷ **Complete the text with the Simple Past or Past Continuous.**

One day while I (Ex.) ....*was walking*.......... (walk) along the road, I (1) .... (see) an old lady.
She (2) .... (wear) a bright red coat and a large black hat, and she (3) ....
(carry) a parrot in a cage. She (4) .... (look) very unusual and I (5) ....
(not want) to talk to her, but she (6) .... (smile) at me and asked me the time.
I (7) .... (tell) her, and she said she (8) .... (be) late for an important
meeting. Then she (9) .... (ask) me the quickest way to get to the White House! While I
was thinking what a strange person she was, she (10) .... (disappear) completely.
I (11) .... (think) it was a dream, but then I (12) .... (see) a red parrot
feather on the ground by my foot!

Pairwork

Work with a partner. Take turns. Ask and answer the following questions:

➤ What were you doing at 8 o'clock yesterday evening?
➤ What was happening in your house at 7 o'clock this morning?
➤ What was the weather like when you woke up this morning?
➤ What was your best friend doing last Saturday morning?
➤ What was everybody in your family wearing yesterday?

Writing

Write a paragraph describing a thunderstorm. Imagine you were outside when the storm began. Think about
the weather: what was happening around you (e.g., describe the trees, the roads, the animals, the sky, your
clothes). Think about what you did and how you felt.

....
....
....
....
....
....
....
....
....
....

4 Present Perfect

Present Perfect

Affirmative	Negative	Question
I have (I've) finished	I have not (haven't) finished	Have I finished?
you have (you've) finished	you have not (haven't) finished	Have you finished?
he has (he's) finished	he has not (hasn't) finished	Has he finished?
she has (she's) finished	she has not (hasn't) finished	Has she finished?
it has (it's) finished	it has not (hasn't) finished	Has it finished?
we have (we've) finished	we have not (haven't) finished	Have we finished?
you have (you've) finished	you have not (haven't) finished	Have you finished?
they have (they've) finished	they have not (haven't) finished	Have they finished?

Short Answers

Yes, I/you have. No, I/you haven't.
Yes, he/she/it has. No, he/she/it hasn't.
Yes, we/you/they have. No, we/you/they haven't.

We form the Present Perfect with *have/has* and the past participle of the main verb. See the Irregular Verbs list on page 132.

We use the Present Perfect to talk about:

➤ something that happened in the past but we don't say exactly when.
They have seen this movie.
She has already had her lunch.

➤ something that happened in the past that has a connection with the present.
He has packed all his things. He's ready to leave now.
I have lost my keys. I can't open the front door.

➤ something that started in the past but has not finished.
I have worked for this company since 2000.
It has been hot for a week.

➤ something that just happened.
We have just finished painting the house.
I've just finished my report. Now we can go for a walk.

Notes

In American English we can also express something that just happened with the Simple Past.
I just saw Ed. = I've just seen Ed.

1 ▸ Complete the sentences with the Present Perfect.

Ex. I ....*have eaten*.......... all my food. *(eat)*

1   The students .... their science projects. (finish)

2   We .... the last bus. We must walk home. (miss)

3   My son .... many different countries. (visit)

4   The farmer .... some of his sheep. (lose)

5   I .... the book you wanted. (find)

6   She .... me a package. (send)

7   The weather .... great this week. (be)

8   They .... where they put their jackets. (forget)

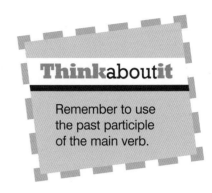

Thinkabout**it**

Remember to use the past participle of the main verb.

2 ▸ Make the sentences negative.

Ex. *I have finished my work.*
      I haven't finished my work.

1   Karen has bought strawberries.
    ....

2   I have seen the Statue of Liberty.
    ....

3   He has washed his car.
    ....

4   They have been friends for years.
    ....

5   Molly has studied in France.
    ....

6   My father has had surgery.
    ....

3 ▸ Write questions.

Ex. *He has won the race.*
      Has he won the race?

1   They have gone to the movies.
    ....

2   You have been to Italy.
    ....

3   He has worked in an office.
    ....

4   Kelly has heard of Mozart.
    ....

5   He has given us our ticket.
    ....

6   The teacher has explained everything.
    ....

4 ▸ Write answers.

Ex. *Has he gained weight? (lose)*
      No, he hasn't. He's lost weight.

1   Have they climbed Mount Everest? (see)
    ....

2   Have you broken your new pen? (lose)
    ....

3   Has your cousin driven to Mexico? (fly)
    ....

4   Has Carol dyed her hair? (wash)
    ....

5   Have astronauts visited the planet Mars? (study)
    ....

6   Has he failed the test? (pass)
    ....

Time Expressions with the Present Perfect

already   never
ever   since
for   yet
just

She's already had lunch. / Has she already had lunch?
Have you ever visited Egypt?
We've lived here for six years.
I've just finished my homework.
I've never met a Chinese person.
We've been married since 1998.
He hasn't gone shopping yet. / Has he gone shopping yet?

Notes

We use *for* with an amount of time.
I have lived here for two years

We use *since* with a specific point in time.
They have attended school since 1996.
I have liked carrots since I was a child.

5 ▶ **Complete the sentences with yet or already.**

Ex. *I haven't finished my breakfast ....yet......... .*

1   Have you .... washed the dishes?
2   They haven't received their grades ....
3   I've .... cooked dinner.
4   Have you made your bed ....?
5   I haven't brushed my teeth ....
6   Anna has .... gone shopping.
7   The bank hasn't lent me any money ....
8   The children have .... gone to bed.

6 ▶ **Complete the sentences with for or since.**

Ex. *They have owned that car ....since......... 2001.*

1   He's worked in that shop .... five years.
2   I've studied English ....two years.
3   Have you had that cat .... it was a kitten?
4   We've been watching this series .... a long time.
5   I haven't seen my cousin .... two months.
6   My grammar has improved .... I started trying harder.
7   We've known each other .... ten years.
8   How have you been .... the last time I saw you?

7 ▶ **Rewrite the sentences. Add have or has in the correct place.**

Ex. *Those boys just bought a new tent.*
     Those boys have just bought a new tent.

1   He already finished his homework.
     ....

2   Lynne made lunch yet?
     ....

3   They lived in Seattle since their child was born.
     ....

4   I never been to China.
     ....

5   Our dog just eaten his food.
     ....

6   Fred ever been to Brazil?
     ....

8 ▷ **Read each situation. Then use the words in parentheses to make a comment in the Present Perfect.**

Ex. *Jason used to go to work by bus. Now he drives to work.*

(buy / a car)

Jason has bought a car.

1   I want some more chocolate but there isn't any left.
(eat / all the chocolate)

....

....

2   He was playing basketball and now he can't walk.
(break / his leg)

....

....

3   The movie starts at 8 o'clock and it's half past
eight now. (miss / the beginning of the movie)

....

....

4   Alice isn't in her office now.
(leave / her office)

....

....

5   I put my watch on the table but it isn't there now.
(lose / my watch)

....

....

6   It's my birthday but my friend hasn't called me.
(forget / my birthday)

....

....

9 ▷ **Complete the sentences with the words from the box.**

already	for	has	have	made	never	remembered	tried	yet

Ex.   They ....*have*............ been to New Zealand lots of times.

1   I have .... to learn Chinese, but it's difficult.

2   .... he given you some money for food?

3   I haven't read this book ....

4   What has she .... for dinner?

5   We've .... washed all the dishes. What's next?

6   Have you .... your report for the meeting?

7   I've worked in this bank .... five years.

8   They've .... seen a gorilla, so let's take them to the zoo.

Have Been and Have Gone

We use *have been* to say that someone went somewhere and came back.
I have been to the Caribbean. It was fantastic!
Have you been to the new Italian restaurant?

We use *have gone* to say that someone went somewhere and is still there.
Penny is not here. She has gone to the bank.
It's very quiet in the house. Have the children gone to school?

10 ▶ Complete the sentences with **have/has been** or **have/has gone**.

Ex. *I'm sick, so my friends* ....*have gone*........ *to the movies without me.*

1 I .... never .... on a boat.

2 "Where .... Helen ....?"
   "She's at the dentist."

3 We .... to Puerto Rico. It's a beautiful island.

4 Tommy .... very sick but he's feeling better now.

5 They waited for you for two hours and now they .... home.

6 .... you ever .... to New York?

11 ▶ Find the extra word and write it on the dotted line.

Ex. *Has he gone already been to the Sydney Opera House?* ......*gone*......

1 What have they to done with their old clothes? ....

2 I've have already seen that movie. ....

3 The game hasn't already started yet. ....

4 Has he written since to his uncle in Australia? ....

5 I've lived here since I was for three. ....

6 We've just worked hard this week. ....

7 The volcano has erupted yet and the local people
   have left their homes. ....

8 I have ever been to Niagara Falls. ....

12 ▶ Find the mistakes and write the sentences correctly.

Ex. *How long was he been a police officer?*
    How long has he been a police officer?

1 We've eat all the cookies.
   ....

2 Has they drunk all the milk?
   ....

3 Have you ever gone to Egypt?
   ....

4 I've ever gone skiing.
   ....

5 The kitten has fell asleep.
   ....

6 She hasn't made her bed already.
   ....

13 ▶ Write the words in the correct order.

Ex. *already / she / the / has / bathroom / cleaned*
    She has already cleaned the bathroom.

1 started / has / college / your / yet / daughter / ?
   ....

2 our / booked / we / yet / trip / haven't
   ....

3 last / I / Suzy / year / written / to / since / haven't
   ....

4 my / put / have / pen / where / you / ?
   ....

5 the / for / they / party / lots of / bought / food / have
   ....

6 already / waited / we / have / three / for / hours
   ....

14 ▶ Match.

Ex.	*What new CDs*	a	I've broken my leg.
1	Have you ever	b	*have you bought since last month?*
2	I can't play soccer because	c	fed the cat yet?
3	Sarah has given	d	been to India?
4	Have they	e	for years.
5	I've already	f	us some books to read.
6	I've had these jeans	g	made lunch.

15 ▶ Complete the sentences in your own words.

Ex. I have just *finished the exercise.*

1 I have never ....

2 I have seen ....

3 My friend has just ....

4 My family has already ....

5 I have been to ....

6 Have you ever ....

Pairwork

Work with a partner. Take turns. Use the Present Perfect to ask and answer questions with the following phrases:

➤ go to Canada
➤ see the Pyramids
➤ eat Indian food
➤ read a play by William Shakespeare
➤ dye your hair
➤ climb Mount Everest
➤ lose a lot of money
➤ win a competition

Writing

1 Write a list of the things you have and haven't done during the last two months.

2 Write a list of the things you have never done.

Review 1 (Units 1-4)

1 ▸ Complete the sentences with do, does, am, is or are.

Ex. ....Do....... you have any children?

1 Nancy and I .... watching TV at the moment.
2 Where .... you and your husband live?
3 .... he listen carefully to the English teacher?
4 .... the computer working properly?
5 I .... listening to everything he says, but I don't understand it all!

6 .... you like working in an office?
7 Steve .... not own a computer.
8 .... you busy at the moment?
9 What .... the letter say?
10 .... I interrupting your conversation?

2 ▸ Complete the sentences with the Simple Present or Present Continuous.

Ex. It ....gets........ dark early in the winter. (get)

1 .... you .... your computer at the moment? (use)
2 She .... how to speak English. (not know)
3 I always .... an umbrella with me when I go out. (take)
4 He .... at a hotel until he finds an apartment. (stay)

5 Today we .... about the environment. (learn)
6 .... he .... a new laptop for his birthday? (want)
7 .... you .... that man outside the house? (know)
8 It usually .... very cold here in the winter. (get)

3 ▸ Choose the correct answer.

Ex. She .... everyone in my family.
   a is knowing   **(b)** knows   **c** know

1 I don't like cherries. I .... strawberries.
   a am preferring   **b** prefer   **c** do prefer

2 He .... a lot of questions today.
   a asks   **b** doesn't ask   **c** is asking

3 Where does she .... to go on Tuesday?
   a wants   **b** want   **c** wanting

4 He .... English very well.
   a speaks   **b** speak   **c** is speaking

5 What .... in your house at the moment?
   a is happening   **b** does happen   **c** happens

6 I .... eggs for breakfast every day.
   a eats   **b** am eating   **c** eat

4 ▸ Complete the sentences with the words from the box.

at	every	in	never
	now	on	twice

Ex. I brush my teeth ....twice........ a day.

1 He listens to music .... day.
2 She is dancing with her boyfriend .... the moment.
3 The sun is shining .... , so we can go out.
4 Grace goes to her music lesson .... Monday evenings.
5 He is very honest and .... tells lies.
6 Janet sits by the fire and reads her book .... the evening.

5 ▶ **Complete the sentences with the Simple Past.**

Ex. I ....*forgot*.......... to give him the message. *(forget)*

1 A long time ago my grandfather .... in Ireland. (live)

2 I .... the play was very interesting. (not think)

3 .... they .... dinner for everyone? (buy)

4 We .... all the answers on the test. (not know)

5 You .... late for work again yesterday. (be)

6 Karen .... a new T-shirt and a pair of jeans for her birthday. (get)

7 .... you .... the snow on the ground this morning? (see)

8 Neil .... the dishes after dinner. (do)

9 She was angry because Sam .... home late. (come)

10 He .... all the milk and now there is none left. (drink)

6 ▶ **Choose the correct answer.**

Ex. *There didn't .... to be any electricity on this island.*
 a *used*   **ⓑ** *use*   **c** *be used*

1 Did you .... walk to work?
 a used   **b** used to   **c** use to

2 We all .... shopping last Saturday.
 a went   **b** used to go   **c** did go

3 .... people live in caves in prehistoric times?
 a Used   **b** Did   **c** Use

4 Where .... his mother meet his father?
 a did   **b** used to   **c** was

5 He .... bring me a souvenir from New York.
 a wasn't   **b** did   **c** didn't

6 My father .... play football when he was young.
 a used to   **b** didn't to   **c** use to

7 .... he use to get into trouble when he was a child?
 a Did   **b** Was   **c** Used

8 I .... my niece three weeks ago.
 a used to see   **b** did see   **c** saw

7 ▶ **Choose the correct answer.**

Ex. *They moved to Australia* (*last*) / *ago year.*

1 She started her last job *in* / *at* 1999.

2 What games did people use to play hundreds of years *before* / *ago* ?

3 Did all the students do their homework *yesterday* / *last day*?

4 My brother used to eat a lot of candy *when* / *as* he was young.

5 I got up very late *before* / *yesterday*.

6 *Two days ago* / *Before two days* she went on vacation.

7 I'm tired today because I worked late *yesterday night* / *last night*.

8 "When did you see her?"
 "The day *before* / *after* yesterday."

8 ▸ **Complete the sentences with the Past Continuous.**

Ex.   Greg ....*was working*........ very hard. *(work)*

1   They .... for the bus for half an hour. (wait)

2   .... he .... around the track all morning? (run)

3   The leaves .... off the trees last week. (fall)

4   It .... all day yesterday. (rain)

5   I .... dinner an hour ago. (make)

6   .... the professor .... on the phone all morning? (speak)

7   We .... pictures for three hours this afternoon. (paint)

8   Mary .... to the radio. (not listen)

9 ▸ **Choose the correct answer.**

Ex.   *I had / was having lunch when you called.*

1   Where *were / did* the children playing last weekend?

2   *Was / Were* he fishing while you were swimming?

3   They *walked / walk* on the beach yesterday.

4   When *did / was* he start to learn English?

5   It *was / was being* hot when we arrived at the airport.

6   He *was talking / was talked* all afternoon.

7   What was your son doing when your wife *arrived / was arriving* home?

8   The cats *sleep / were sleeping* while the dogs were barking.

10 ▸ **Write sentences. Use the Simple Past, Past Continuous and when, while or and to join the two parts.**

Ex.   *we put on our swimsuits / then we go swimming*
      We put on our swimsuits and then we
      ...
      went swimming.
      ...

1   I wash the dishes / I break a glass

....

....

2   she listen to music / I arrive

....

....

3   the sun shine / I walk to the store

....

....

4   the computer crash / I use it

....

....

5   you talk to someone / I see you

....

....

6   first she buy ingredients / then she make a cake

....

....

7   Adam play football / break his leg

....

....

8   they go to bed at 2 a.m. / wake up at noon

....

....

11 Complete the second sentence so that it has a similar meaning to the first sentence. Use the word in parentheses in your answer.

Ex. *I saw Angela last week. (since)*
I haven't ......*seen Angela since*........ *last week.*

1 We gave them a lot of chocolate and they ate it all. (have)
They .... all the chocolate
we gave them.

2 Mark bought a new motorcycle yesterday. (just)
Mark .... a new motorcycle.

3 This is the best book I have ever read. (never)
I .... such a good book.

4 He can't find his keys. (lost)
He .... his keys.

5 John isn't here. He is at the doctor. (has)
John .... to
the doctor.

6 Don't buy bread. Jenny bought some. (already)
Jenny .... some bread.

7 I met Maria in 1999. (known)
I .... 1999.

8 I must work for another two hours. (finished)
I .... my work yet.

12 Complete the sentences with the words from the box.

> already   always   ever   for
> just   never   since (x2)   yet

Ex. *Oh, no! There goes the bus. We've* ......*just*...... *missed it!*

1 Why haven't you written to me ....?

2 I'm not hungry. I've .... had lunch.

3 I haven't seen you .... ages.

4 I haven't spoken French .... I was in college.

5 Have you .... eaten Thai noodles?

6 They've lived there .... 2000.

7 Astronauts have .... wanted to go to Mars.

8 We've .... been to the Great Wall of China.

13 Find the extra word and write it on the dotted line.

Ex. *Have you ever did been to Los Angeles?* ....*did*........

1 We've already eaten yet so we aren't hungry now. ....

2 Have you lived here for since you were born? ....

3 They have to seen the movie already. ....

4 Have you ever been wanted to go to Australia? ....

5 Has he remembered to bring his cell phone already? ....

6 Who has been on vacation since this year? ....

7 Laura has always bought some cherries for you. ....

8 Has he been met your parents? ....

5 Simple Past & Present Perfect

HE STUDIED COMPUTER SCIENCE IN COLLEGE, BUT HE'S BROKEN THE SERVER FOUR TIMES THIS MONTH!

MAIN COMPUTER ROOM

Simple Past

I finished the report an hour ago.
You didn't finish the report an hour ago.
Did she finish the report an hour ago?

I bought a new CD.
You didn't buy a new CD.
Did he buy a new CD?

We use the Simple Past to talk about:

➤ something that happened at a specified time in the past.
James lost his keys yesterday.
Kerry called Tina this morning.

➤ something that started and finished in the past.
They moved to Chicago four years ago.
She went to Hawaii last year.

1 ▷ **Complete the sentences with the Simple Past.**

Ex. *They ....visited.......... their daughter in California last summer. (visit)*

1   .... you .... the paintings by Picasso at the
    art gallery? (see)

2   Where .... you when I called your house? (be)

3   He .... a salad for lunch today. (have)

4   I .... a dog in my yard this morning. (find)

5   They .... the answers to any of my questions. (not know)

6   My dog .... three cats in the park yesterday. (chase)

7   Tom .... his project last week. (finish)

8   .... Mike at work yesterday afternoon? (be)

Present Perfect

I have washed the car.
You haven't washed the car.
Has he washed the car?

I have drunk all the milk.
You haven't drunk all the milk.
Has she drunk all the milk?

We use the Present Perfect to talk about:

➤ something that happened in the past but we don't say when.
They've been to Italy.
She's lost her English book.

➤ something that started and finished in the past but is still important now.
I've lost my wallet so I can't pay for dinner.
His car has broken down so he can't take us to the airport.

➤ something that started in the past but hasn't finished yet.
I have worked here for two years.
She has lived in Texas since she was born.

---

2 ▶ **Complete the sentences with the Present Perfect.**

Ex.   *Greg* .....*has learned*..... *a lot about chemistry. (learn)*

1   We .... a new car. Do you like it? (buy)

2   He .... of a new way to earn money. (think)

3   Scientists .... a way to make people live longer. (find)

4   Astronomers .... some new stars. (discover)

5   I .... all my lunch because I don't feel well. (not eat)

6   .... he .... from his friend since
    he moved to Chicago? (hear)

7   Bob .... his glasses. Now he can't see very well. (break)

8   .... you ever .... in Italy? (drive)

Thinkaboutit

We use the past participle
of the main verb for all
forms of the Present
Perfect.

---

3 ▶ **Write SP if the verb is in the Simple Past or PP if the verb is in the Present Perfect.**

Ex.   *He went to the gym every day last week.* _SP_

      He's become much stronger over the past few months. _PP_

1   They went to a party last Saturday. _____   5   We've visited lots of countries in Europe. _____

2   Did you have a good time at the picnic? _____   6   They didn't have fish for dinner. _____

3   I haven't eaten this morning. _____   7   She hasn't been to the new stadium yet. _____

4   Have his parents given him his new bicycle yet? _____   8   I went for a long walk this morning. _____

---

4 ▶ **Write sentences with the Simple Past or the Present Perfect.**

Ex.   *Nina / go / to China / last year*   *She / never / travel / by plane*
      Nina went to China last year.   *She has never traveled by plane.*
      ....

1   I / spend / a lot of money / since my birhday   4   I / be / to the theater / twice this year
    ....

2   She / never / see / a giraffe   5   Astronauts / land / on the moon / in 1969
    ....

3   He / exercise / at the gym / this morning   6   Lisa / know / Ken / since she was a child
    ....

5 ▶ **Write questions.**

Ex. ...*Did the car break down when you were on the highway?*...

Yes, the car broke down when we were on the highway.

1 ....

No, he's never flown in a plane.

2 ....

Yes, I waited for my friend outside the supermarket.

3 ....

Yes, I've studied for all my finals.

4 ....

No, she didn't know the party was on Saturday.

5 ....

Yes, I've bought Liz a new bag for her birthday.

6 ....

Yes, I saw the new library yesterday.

6 ▶ **Complete the sentences with the Simple Past or the Present Perfect.**

Ex. I ......*have had*...... a car since I ....*started*........ *working last year. (have, start)*

1 I .... Jenny since we .... in high school. (know, be)

2 I .... my friend two e-mails this week but she .... yet. (send, not reply)

3 What .... to your hair since the last time I .... you? (you/do, see)

4 We .... a cake for Gina's birthday already but we .... her a present yet.
(make, not buy)

5 Last week Al .... me a new CD, so I .... him a thank-you note today. (give, write)

6 I .... to the doctor twice since Monday, but he .... there is nothing wrong
with me. (be, say)

7 ▶ **Choose the correct answer.**

Ex. *Has he ever (been) / went to Asia?*

1 I've *never / ever* noticed that building before.

2 She *knew / has known* him for ten years.

3 I *haven't / didn't* finished yet.

4 I *ate / have eaten* lunch before I went shopping.

5 Has he *meet / met* the new student?

6 We have known Jim *since / for* 1999.

8 **Match.**

Ex. I met him in high school   a   since he moved to Boston?

1   In college he drank lots of soda,   b   but she's recently become a vegetarian.

2   Has Ed e-mailed you   c   *and we've been good friends for eight years*

3   He spent his childhood in Japan   d   since they moved here five years ago?

4   Have they lived in the same apartment   e   but she's been married for almost five years now.

5   Ten years ago she was single   f   but since then he's lived in five other countries.

6   She ate meat in college   g   but he's recently become a coffee drinker.

9 **Complete the sentences with the words from the box.**

ago	for	has	just	last week	never	since	speak	spoken

Ex. We've ....*never*............... been to Africa.

1   I've .... finished washing the dishes. Can I do anything else for you?

2   .... he read all those computer magazines yet?

3   Did you .... English when you were four years old?

4   They moved into a new house two months ....

5   Have you .... to your friends about the trip?

6   We've lived in Japan .... 2001.

7   I met Valerie ....

8   She's driven a jeep .... two years.

10 **Find the mistakes and write the sentences correctly.**

Ex. *I've never wake up so late before.*
     I've never woken up so late before.

1   When you been small, did you like spinach?

     ....

2   Has you ever been to the desert in Arizona?

     ....

3   They've did built a new library since I moved here.

     ....

4   I've wanted to go to India for I was a child.

     ....

5   My son already seen that movie.

     ....

6   What have you do when you were at the park?

     ....

11 ▶ **Choose the correct answer.**

Ex. *The train has .... arrived at the station.*

   (**a**) *just*   **b** *always*   **c** *never*

1   We .... to Rio de Janeiro several times.
     a been   **b** have went   **c** have been

2   .... you watch the news last night?
     a Have   **b** Did   **c** Were

3   How long .... known about this?
     a did you   **b** have   **c** have you

4   He never .... eggs when he was young.
     a has eaten   **b** ate   **c** did eat

5   I .... you since the first time I met you.
     a have liked   **b** like   **c** liked

6   We've .... asked the coach about the things
     we don't understand.
     a ever   **b** since   **c** already

12 ▶ **Find the extra word in each sentence and write it on the dotted line.**

Ex. *He's just eaten a huge pizza yet.* ....*yet*..........

1   They have thought that the concert was fantastic. ....

2   Has your team did won all their games this year? ....

3   Lots of animals they have died in the forest fire. ....

4   When since did you break your arm? ....

5   I've did forgotten your name. ....

6   Did you go to school when you have were four years old? ....

7   What has been happened since I left this morning? ....

8   Our neighbors have came back from their vacation yesterday. ....

13 ▶ **Choose the correct answer.**

Ex. *Julia has had short hair* (*since*) / *when she was eighteen.*

1   Kate has *ever / just* painted her living room blue.

2   Where did they go on vacation *last / before* summer?

3   Did you know Bill two years *ago / since*?

4   I haven't been to Boston *when / since* I was a young boy.

5   My computer hasn't worked *since / for* weeks.

6   Rock and roll has been popular *when / since* the 1960s.

7   Did he write songs thirty years *since / ago*?

8   Have you *always / already* wanted to race motorcycles?

Pairwork

Work with a partner. Take turns. Ask and answer the following questions.

- ➤ When did you have your first English lesson?
- ➤ How long have you lived in your current home?
- ➤ What did you do last night?
- ➤ Have you ever been to another country?
- ➤ Where did you go on vacation last year?
- ➤ Have you ever organized a big party?
- ➤ What did you eat for lunch yesterday?
- ➤ What music have you listened to this week?
- ➤ What have you watched on TV this week?

Writing

Write a letter to your friend telling him/her about recent events in your life. For example, you can write about a place you have visited, a person you have met or something you have learned. You can describe something happy, exciting, unusual, dangerous or funny. Include verbs in the Simple Past and the Present Perfect.

Dear ....,

....

....

....

....

....

....

....

....

....

....

....

Best wishes,

....

Present Continuous – Future Meaning

I am having a party next Saturday.
You are not leaving tomorrow.
Is he coming with us tonight?

We can use the Present Continuous to talk about plans and arrangements for the future.

We're meeting him outside the restaurant later.
They are going on a trip tomorrow.

Lisa's things to do

Monday: clean the house
Tuesday: bake a cake
Wednesday: go shopping
Thursday: exercise at the gym
Friday: wash hair
Saturday: get married!
Sunday: go on honeymoon

1 ▶ **Write sentences.**

Ex. *She's cleaning the house on Monday.* ....

1 ....

2 ....

3 ....

4 ....

5 ....

6 ....

2 ▶ **Complete the sentences with the Present Continuous.**

Ex. What ....*are you doing*................ this weekend? *(you / do)*

1 Nancy .... with her lawyer next week. *(not meet)*

2 My neighbors .... a party on Saturday. *(have)*

3 Luke and Gina .... on vacation this year. *(not go)*

4 .... you to the airport tomorrow? *(Mark / take)*

5 I .... a new job in June. *(start)*

6 What time .... on Monday? *(our friends / arrive)*

The Future with Will

Affirmative
I will (I'll) work
you will (you'll) work
he will (he'll) work
she will (she'll) work
it will (it'll) work
we will (we'll) work
you will (you'll) work
they will (they'll) work

Negative
I will not (won't) work
you will not (won't) work
he will not (won't) work
she will not (won't) work
it will not (won't) work
we will not (won't) work
you will not (won't) work
they will not (won't) work

Question
Will I work?
Will you work?
Will he work?
Will she work?
Will it work?
Will we work?
Will you work?
Will they work?

Short Answers

Yes, I/you will.
Yes, he/she/it will.
Yes, we/you/they will.

No, I/you won't.
No, he/she/it won't.
No, we/you/they won't.

We use the Future with *Will*:

➤ for predictions about the future.
*You will have lots of children and a long,
happy life.*

➤ for decisions made at the time of speaking.
This dress is perfect! I'll buy it.

➤ for promises.
I won't be late. I promise.

➤ for offers.
*I'll take you to the airport.
We'll do the shopping for you.*

➤ for threats and warnings.
Look out! You'll fall into that hole!

Notes

Shall is a polite form of *will*. We can use
it in questions with *I* and *we* when we
want to offer to do something or when
we are suggesting something.

Shall I get you a cup of coffee?
Shall we have lunch together?

---

3 ▷ **Complete the sentences with will or shall and the word in parentheses.**

Ex. *They ....will bring.......... us a souvenir from their trip to Asia. (bring)*

1   He .... the best athlete in the school when he's older. (be)

2   We .... you move your furniture tomorrow. (help)

3   He .... late because he's taking a taxi. (not be)

4   .... we .... that new French restaurant
    across from the park tonight? (try)

5   They .... really nice in their new clothes. (look)

6   I .... to the movies with them tonight. I ....
    home with you. (not go, stay)

7   Don't worry. You .... your driving test. (pass)

8   .... I .... you with the cooking? (help)

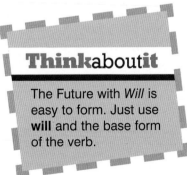

Thinkabout**it**

The Future with *Will* is
easy to form. Just use
will and the base form
of the verb.

4 ▶ **Write questions and answers with will.**

Ex. *you / be / on vacation / in March / ? / be / at home*
Will you be on vacation in March? No, I won't. I'll be at home.
....

1 you / carry / these heavy books / ? / carry / that box

....

2 we / arrive / at the hotel / in the morning / ? / arrive / in the afternoon

....

3 he / buy / those new jeans / ? / look for / a new suit

....

4 the concert tickets / be / expensive / ? / be / cheap

....

5 the sun / shine / tomorrow / ? / rain

....

6 he / have / time for lunch / tomorrow / ? / eat / in his office

....

Be Going To

Affirmative	**Negative**	**Question**
I am (I'm) going to work	I am not (I'm not) going to work	Am I going to work?
you are (you're) going to work	you are not (aren't) going to work	Are you going to work?
he is (he's) going to work	he is not (isn't) going to work	Is he going to work?
she is (she's) going to work	she is not (isn't) going to work	Is she going to work?
it is (it's) going to work	it is not (isn't) going to work	Is it going to work?
we are (we're) going to work	we are not (aren't) going to work	Are we going to work?
you are (you're) going to work	you are not (aren't) going to work	Are you going to work?
they are (they're) going to work	they are not (aren't) going to work	Are they going to work?

Short Answers

Yes, I am.	No, I'm not.
Yes, you are.	No, you aren't.
Yes, he/she/it is.	No, he/she/it isn't.
Yes, we/you/they are.	No, we/you/they aren't.

We use *be going to* to talk about:

➤ plans and arrangements in the near future.
We are going to try that new Italian restaurant tomorrow.
He is going to take his driving test next week.

➤ something we know is going to happen because we have evidence.
He's driving too fast. He's going to crash!
I didn't study. I'm going to fail the exam.

Notes

We can use *be going to* or the Present Continuous (future meaning) for things we have arranged:
I'm going to meet him on Saturday.
I'm meeting him on Saturday.

5 Complete the sentences with the correct form of be going to and a verb from the box.

be   buy   clean   go   see   snow   study

Ex.   I think I ....*am going to be*........ nervous at the interview.

1   We .... a play tomorrow evening.

2   He .... his house later this afternoon.

3   The students .... English next year.

4   I .... a new DVD player this weekend.

5   We .... to Australia next month.

6   It's very cold. I think it .... tonight.

6 Write what is going to happen. Many answers are possible. Use your imagination.

Ex.   I have a swimsuit and a towel.
      I am going to go swimming.
      ....

1   We are buying snacks, soda and party hats.
    ....

2   She has money and is at the grocery store.
    ....

3   I have eaten too much ice cream and I don't feel well.
    ....

4   He has some flour, sugar and eggs.
    ....

5   He has a brush, some paint and a ladder.
    ....

6   The children are tired and they are wearing pajamas.
    ....

7 Write questions.

Ex.   Nicole is cleaning the house.
      Is Nicole cleaning the house?
      ....

1   It's going to rain before it gets dark.
    ....

2   You're painting the house next week.
    ....
    ....

3   Bob is meeting with his lawyer next week.
    ....
    ....

4   We will be in trouble when the police arrive.
    ....
    ....

5   They're visiting the museum on Saturday morning.
    ....
    ....

8 Make the sentences negative.

Ex.   They are going to pass their exams.
      They aren't going to pass their exams.
      ....

1   He is working tomorrow.
    ....

2   She's acting in the play this evening.
    ....
    ....

3   We're visiting my parents in Florida next week.
    ....
    ....

4   They're going to buy a very expensive car.
    ....
    ....

5   She'll be home before 9 o'clock.
    ....
    ....

Time Expressions with the Future

in a minute	next Monday	next year	tomorrow
in a while	next month	this afternoon	tonight
later	next week	this evening	soon

He's going to finish in a minute.
I'm going to start work next Monday.
We'll go and see her tomorrow.

---

9 ► **Complete the sentences in your own words.**

Ex. *This weekend I'm going to* ....*go to the*................
.....*art museum.*...

1   Soon my friend will ....
....

2   Next year I'll ....
....

3   This evening I'm going to ....
....

4   Tomorrow I'm ....
....

5   In ten years I'll ....
....

6   Next summer I'm ....
....

10 ► **Choose the correct answer.**

Ex. *"What would you like to eat?" "........ a burger, please."*

   a *I'm going to have*   **b** *I'm having*   ⓒ *I'll have*

1   I promise .... never leave you.
   a I'm going to   b I'll   c I'm

2   She .... twenty-seven next year.
   a will be   **b** is being   **c** is going

3   He .... a new computer on Saturday.
   a is going to buy   **b** buys   **c** will buys

4   Look at that tree! It .... fall down!
   a will   **b** is   **c** is going to

5   The plane .... at 9 o'clock this evening.
   a is going to leaving   **b** is leaving   **c** will leaving

6   I .... the doctor the day after tomorrow.
   a am seeing   **b** going see   **c** will seeing

---

11 ► **Find the mistakes and write the sentences correctly.**

Ex. *Will I help you with those suitcases?*
   Shall I help you with those suitcases?..............

1   I promise I'm being home by 11 o'clock.
....

2   He won't to help me paint the bedroom.
....

3   They're going learn English grammar.
....

4   Her friend will coming to visit later.
....

5   Is she start her new job next week?
....

6   My dinner party goes to be fantastic!
....

12 ▶ Find the extra word in each sentence and write it on the dotted line.

Ex.   *I'm going to be wear my new T-shirt to the party.* ....*be*....

1   Will you to do the laundry? ....

2   What are you going making for dinner? ....

3   Is he going to be drive to Boston this evening? ....

4   He won't not come to my party. ....

5   They're be watching the game on TV on Saturday evening. ....

6   I'm going to shopping in the morning. ....

Pairwork

Work with a partner. Talk about your future. Take turns.
Ask and answer about:

➤ your home   ➤ your job
➤ your family   ➤ your hobbies

Writing

Write a paragraph about what you think the world will be like one hundred years from now. Use language from this unit to describe houses, pollution, cars, clothes and any other ideas that you have.

....
....
....
....
....
....
....
....
....
....
....
....
....
....
....
....

7 Can, Could & Be Able To

CAN YOU BUY ME A SANDWICH FOR LUNCH?
... AND COULD I PAY YOU BACK TOMORROW?

Can

Affirmative
I/you can play
he/she/it can play
we/you/they can play

Negative
I/you cannot (can't) play
he/she/it cannot (can't) play
we/you/they cannot (can't) play

Question
Can I/you play?
Can he/she/it play?
Can we/you/they play?

Short Answers

Yes, I/you can.   No, I/you can't.
Yes, he/she/it can.   No, he/she/it can't.
Yes, we/you/they can.   No, we/you/they can't.

Can is a modal verb. It has only one form and does not add
-s with *he*, *she* or *it*. We use the base form of a verb after it.

We use *can*:

➤ to talk about ability in the present.
  He can speak Spanish.
  She can run fast.

➤ to ask for and give/refuse permission in the present
  and future.
  "Can I come in now?" "Yes, you can."
  "Can I stay out late tomorrow?" "No, you can't."

➤ to ask for something (request).
  Can you pass me the salt, please?

Notes

When we want to talk about ability in the future or
with the Present Perfect, we use *be able to* instead
of *can*. See page 47 for more information.

---

1 ▶ Complete the sentences with **can** and the verbs from the box.

| borrow | buy | explain | mail | paint | sing | speak | watch | work |

Ex. *He* .....*can speak*..... *Russian.*

1 You .... at home today.

2 The teacher .... the grammar rules.

3 My daughter .... very well. She wants to be an artist.

4 .... you .... this letter for me, please?

5 .... I .... a new sofa with the money you gave me?

6 She is in a rock group because she .... very well.

7 .... we .... a documentary this evening?

8 You .... my new book.

Think about it

Can always stays
the same – you don't
add **-s** with **he**,
she and **it**.

44

2 ▶ **Complete the sentences with can or can't.**

Ex.   *Babies* ....*can't*....... *drive cars.*

1   Lucy .... speak French because she's lived in Paris for years.

2   Plants .... grow without water.

3   Tony .... lift that box because he's very strong.

4   I .... play chess because I don't understand the rules.

5   Cats .... climb trees.

6   Doctors .... cure every illness in the world.

3 ▶ **Write sentences making requests or asking for permission.**

Ex.   *borrow your car*
      Can I borrow your car?
      ....

1   use your phone   4   contact you later
    ....

2   send me a message   5   meet me at the bank
    ....

3   write me a letter   6   join you for lunch
    ....

Could

Affirmative

I/you could swim
he/she/it could swim
we/you/they could swim

Negative

I/you could not (couldn't) swim
he/she/it could not (couldn't) swim
we/you/they could not (couldn't) swim

Question

Could I/you swim?
Could he/she/it swim?
Could we/you/they swim?

Short Answers

Yes, I/you could.   No, I/you couldn't.
Yes, he/she/it could.   No, he/she/it couldn't.
Yes, we/you/they could.   No, we/you/they couldn't.

Like *can*, *could* is a modal verb. It has only one form and does not add -*s* with *he*, *she* or *it*. We use the base form of a verb after it.

We use *could*:

➤ to talk about past ability.
  He could ride his bike very fast when he was a boy.

➤ to ask for permission in the present or the future.
  Could I use your pen for a minute?
  Could I leave work early tomorrow?

➤ to ask for something politely (request).
  Could you take me home, please?

4 ► Write **A** for ability, **P** for permission or **R** for request.

Ex. *Could he drive a car when he was eighteen?* _A_

1 Could you help me with my report later? ___
2 Could you buy me a newspaper when you go out, please? ___
3 Could I use your computer? ___
4 Could you wait for me for ten minutes? ___
5 Could you speak English when you were four? ___
6 Could she swim fast a few years ago? ___
7 Could I borrow your bike this afternoon? ___
8 Could he dance well when he was a boy? ___

5 ► Write polite requests using **could**.

Ex. *You are thirsty.*
Could I have a drink of water, please?

1 You need help with your report.
....

2 You don't have a pen but your friend has two.
....

3 You need some money for a taxi.
....

4 You're at your friend's house and you want to make a phone call.
....

5 You have met a Japanese teacher and you want to learn how to speak Japanese.
....

6 ► Write questions and answers.

Ex. *he / ride a motorcyle / young (ride a bicycle)*
Could he ride a motorcyle when he was young?
No, he couldn't. He could ride a bicycle.

1 she / swim / a little girl (make beautiful sand castles)
....
....

2 they / cook / young (help their mother bake a cake)
....
....

3 your granddaughter / read / ten years ago (write her name)
....
....

4 astronauts / go to Saturn / in 1990 (walk on the moon)
....
....

5 people / build houses with bricks / thousands of years ago (make houses with mud)
....
....

Be Able To

Affirmative	Negative	Question
I am able to visit	I am not (I'm not) able to visit	Am I able to visit?
you are able to visit	you are not (aren't) able to visit	Are you able to visit?
he is able to visit	he is not (isn't) able to visit	Is he able to visit?
she is able to visit	she is not (isn't) able to visit	Is she able to visit?
it is able to visit	it is not (isn't) able to visit	Is it able to visit?
we are able to visit	we are not (aren't) able to visit	Are we able to visit?
you are able to visit	you are not (aren't) able to visit	Are you able to visit?
they are able to visit	they are not (aren't) able to visit	Are they able to visit?

Short Answers

Yes, I am.	No, I'm not.
Yes, you are.	No, you aren't.
Yes, he/she/it is.	No, he/she/it isn't.
Yes, we/you/they are.	No, we/you/they aren't.

We can use *be able to* in several tenses.

Simple Present – *I am able to, you are able to, he is able to*, etc.
Simple Past – *I was able to, you were able to, he was able to*, etc.
Present Perfect – *I have been able to, you have been able to, he has been able to*, etc.
Future with *Will* – *I will be able to, you will be able to, he will be able to*, etc.

We use *be able to* to talk about ability in the past, present or future.
I was able to go to her dinner party last weekend.
He is able to speak French.
They will be able to visit next Wednesday.

---

7 ▶ **Rewrite the sentences using the Simple Past of be able to.**

Ex.   *I could do handstands when I was younger.*
      I was able to do handstands when I was younger.

1   Could your mother swim when she was a little girl?

      ....

2   I couldn't use the computer software.

      ....

3   Could you read at the age of five?

      ....

4   She could play the guitar very well.

      ....

5   The twins couldn't walk until they were three.

      ....

6   Could they always play basketball well?

      ....

8 ▶ **Choose the correct answer.**

Ex. *My grandmother* is able to / (could) *speak Spanish when she was a girl.*

1 *Could I / Was I able to go to Mexico next year?*

2 *Can he / Has he been able to go to the movies with his friends tonight?*

3 *Was I able to / Can I watch that DVD with you tonight?*

4 *Could you / Will you able to help me with these bags, please?*

5 *I can't / couldn't lift heavy things now but I could when I was young.*

6 *He was able to / can play with his friends everyday when he was a boy.*

9 ▶ **Complete the sentences with the words from the box.**

| can | can't | could | couldn't | has been able to | were ... able to | will be able to |

Ex. *Doctors* .... *can't* .... *make people live forever.*

1 Do you think astronauts .... fly to Saturn in the near future?

2 I .... dance well but I am not good at singing.

3 He .... come to my party last Saturday because he was ill.

4 .... you .... swim fast when you were a teenager?

5 She .... speak four languages since she was a child.

6 I can't speak Japanese well, but I .... understand a little when I was in Tokyo last year.

Pairwork

Work with a partner. Take turns. Think of three things you want and request them from your partner.

Writing

1 Write a short paragraph about your abilities. Say what you can or can't do now and what you could or couldn't do ten years ago.

2 Write a short paragraph about what people will be able to do and not be able to do in the year 2100.

Must

Affirmative	Negative
I/you must pay	I/you must not pay
he/she/it must pay	he/she/it must not pay
we/you/they must pay	we/you/they must not pay

Must is a modal verb. It has only one form and does not add -*s* with *he*, *she* or *it*. We use the base form of a verb after it.

We use *must*:

➤ to talk about obligation in the present or in the future.
You must wear a seatbelt in the car.

➤ to say that something is necessary in the present or in the future (necessity).
I must finish this report today.

We use *must not*:

➤ to talk about prohibition in the present or in the future.
You must not speak to your boss like that.

Notes

The form *mustn't* and questions with *must* are not common in American English. We usually use *have to* in questions of obligation. (see page 50).

1 ➤ **Write N for necessity, O for obligation and P for prohibition.**

Ex. *You must arrive at work on time.* _O_

1   They must not eat in class. ___
2   You must not smoke in the doctor's waiting room. ___
3   I must study hard if I want to pass the exams. ___
4   You must not talk in the library. ___
5   We must not make noise because the baby is sleeping. ___
6   He must learn to drive before he can start his new job. ___
7   You must not talk on the phone for so long. ___
8   You must water the plants or they'll die. ___

49

2 ▸ Complete the sentences with **must** or **must not** to make office rules.

Ex. *You* ....*must*....... *work hard.*

1   You .... recycle old paper.

2   You .... leave your computer on all night.

3   You .... keep the office neat.

4   You .... wear jeans to work.

5   You .... be on time for meetings.

6   You .... eat food at your desk. Please eat in the cafeteria.

Have To / Don't Have To

Affirmative
I/you have to go
he/she/it has to go
we/you/they have to go

Negative
I/you do not (don't) have to go
he/she/it does not (doesn't) have to go
we/you/they do not (don't) have to go

Question
Do I/you have to go?
Does he/she/it have to go?
Do we/you/they have to go?

Short Answers

Yes, I/you do.   No, I/you don't.
Yes, he/she/it does.   No, he/she/it doesn't.
Yes, we/you/they do.   No, we/you/they don't.

We use the base form of the verb after *have to* and *don't have to*. After *he*, *she* and *it*, we use the forms *has to* and *doesn't have to*.

We can use *have to* as follows:

Simple Present – *I have to, you have to, he has to*, etc.
Simple Past – *I had to, you had to, he had to*, etc.
Present Perfect – *I have had to, you have had to, he has had to*, etc.
Future with *Will* – *I will have to, you will have to, he will have to*, etc.

We use *have to* to talk about obligation.
I have to do a lot of work tonight.

We use *don't have to* for things that are not necessary.
I don't have to buy any bread. I bought some this morning.

3 ▸ Write questions.

Ex.   *Do I have to leave now?* ....

   Yes, you have to leave now.

1   ....

   Yes, you have to write the article before you go home.

2   ....

   No, they don't have to go out now.

3   ....

   Yes, we have to do what the manager says.

4   ....

   Yes, he has to pass a written test to get a driver's license?

5   ....

   Yes, she has to stay home this evening.

6   ....

   No, he doesn't have to pay for the meal.

4 ▶ **Write questions and answers.**

Ex. *I / cook a chicken / tonight (make a salad)*
Do I have to cook a chicken tonight?
No, you don't. You have to make a salad.

1   the students / read poetry / today (write an essay)

....

....

2   he / pay / the phone bill / today (go to the bank)

....

....

3   we / get up early / on Saturdays (get up early on Mondays)

....

....

4   she / lose weight (eat more fruit and vegetables)

....

....

5   we / look after the baby / later (feed the dog)

....

....

5 ▶ **Complete the sentences with the correct form of have to or don't have to and the verbs from the box.**

buy	clean	cook	get up	help	make	wash

Ex. *I ....don't have to cook.......... dinner tonight because we're going to eat out.*

1   He .... at 6 o'clock every morning to go to work.

2   Jenny .... the house today. She cleaned it yesterday.

3   You .... me – I can do it myself.

4   I will .... a cake because it's my husband's birthday tomorrow.

5   Those clothes are very dirty. You'll .... them now!

6   You .... any food. I went shopping this morning.

6 ▶ **Match.**

Ex. *It was hot yesterday.*   a   I have to study for my exams.

1   My car has a flat tire.   b   We don't have to get up at 6 o'clock.

2   I fed the dog an hour ago.   c   I'll have to go to work by bus tomorrow.

3   My brother fixed my car.   d   *I didn't have to wear a jacket.*

4   We are on vacation this week.   e   I don't have to feed him again until this evening.

5   I feel ill.   f   I don't have to go to the mechanic today.

6   I can't come out with you this evening.   g   I'll have to go to the doctor this evening.

Must / Have To and Must Not / Don't Have To

Must and *must not* are stronger in meaning than *have to* and *don't have to*.
I must go to the doctor. (I am very ill.)
I have to fix the car. (If I don't, my wife will be angry.)

Must and *have to* have very similar meanings.
I must go now.
I have to go now.

Must not and *don't have to* have very different meanings.
This report is top secret. You must not tell anyone. (prohibition)
You don't have to wash your car today. You can do it tomorrow. (lack of obligation)

---

7 ▸ **Choose the correct answer.**

Ex. *I* ⟨don't have to⟩ / must not *go to work tomorrow because I'm on vacation.*

1 The children *don't have to / must not* play games in the classroom.

2 He *must not / doesn't have to* make his lunch. He can buy lunch in the cafeteria.

3 You *don't have to / must not* forget to brush your teeth before you go to bed.

4 She *must / must not* ride her motorcycle without a helmet.

5 You *must not / don't have to* steal or tell lies. It's wrong.

6 Children *have to / don't have to* eat healthy food and get plenty of sleep.

---

8 ▸ **Find the mistakes and write the sentences correctly.**

Ex. *You have wear a hat when it's very cold.*
     You have to wear a hat when it's very cold. ....

1 We don't must be rude to other people.
   ....

2 He has to finishes the job before 5 o'clock.
   ....

3 I have remember to lock the door when I go out.
   ....

4 Sarah must visit the dentist last week.
   ....

5 Did you have to helped your son with his homework?
   ....

6 What time do they have to been home this evening?
   ....

7 We must not using Brian's computer without his permission.
   ....

8 I must leave work early two days ago.
   ....

9 ▶ **Find the extra word in each sentence and write it on the dotted line.**

Ex. *They must not not forget to wash their hands.* ....*not*.......

1 Does he have to had learn all the grammar by tomorrow? ....

2 We must not to read magazines at work. ....

3 When I was young, I have had to walk to school. ....

4 She must to call her parents tonight. ....

5 Doctors must be try hard to help all their patients. ....

6 Did you have to must eat all your dinner when you were young? ....

10 ▶ **Complete the sentences in your own words. Use must and have to.**

Ex. *It's snowing. I* ...*must wear my coat and boots.*...

1 I'm tired. I ....

2 My grades aren't very good. I ....

3 I haven't finished all my work. I ....

4 My desk is messy; my boss is unhappy with me. I ....

5 The cat is hungry. I ....

6 I don't have any money. I ....

7 Too much junk food isn't good for me. I ....

8 It's very hot outside. I ....

Pairwork

Work with a partner. Tell your partner three things you are obliged to do – either at home, at school or at work. Then tell your partner three things you know you must not do when you live in or visit a big city.

Writing

1 Write a short paragraph about what students must and must not do if they want to get good grades.

2 Write a list of the things you have to do and don't have to do next weekend.

Review 2 (Units 5-8)

1 ▸ **Complete the sentences with the Simple Past or the Present Perfect.**

Ex. We .... *left* .... the party at 11 o'clock. (leave)

1 Five years ago we .... to Spain on vacation. (go)

2 I .... weight since November. (lose)

3 What .... at your last job? (you / do)

4 She .... an operation since I last saw her. (have)

5 What .... last night? (they / eat)

6 They .... to four concerts this summer. (be)

7 What .... since you got up this morning? (you / eat)

8 We .... at the library on Tuesday. (be)

2 ▸ **Complete the sentences with the words from the box.**

> ago   always   for   month   never
> since   last   yesterday   yet

Ex. We've been friends .... *for* .... years.

1 She has .... seen an alligator.

2 He walked to the swimming pool ....

3 Have they finished cleaning the car ....?

4 We went to the bookstore at 7 o'clock .... night.

5 I haven't seen George ....1999.

6 They've .... wanted to see that rock group perform on stage.

7 I've lived in Houston since I moved there four years ....

8 I met my mother's cousin for the first time last ....

3 ▸ **Choose the correct answer.**

Ex. We .... the house last week.
   a have sold   **b** were selling   **(c)** sold

1 My niece .... twice since Tuesday.
   a called   **b** has called   **c** have called

2 Have you ever .... on a camel?
   a ride   **b** rode   **c** ridden

3 What .... he say to the boss yesterday?
   a has   **b** was   **c** did

4 .... he been to Korea and Japan?
   a Has   **b** Did   **c** Have

5 They've always .... good students.
   a be   **b** were   **c** been

6 Did you .... to the art gallery when you visited New York?
   a went   **b** go   **c** gone

7 Have you ever .... the color of your hair?
   a changed   **b** change   **c** changes

8 Is that the car you .... since you were sixteen?
   a had   **b** has had   **c** have had

4 ▸ **Find the extra word in each sentence and write it on the dotted line.**

Ex. We did went to the movies last Saturday night. ...... *did* ......

1 I have already made the beds and cleaned the kitchen now. ....

2 We've have just won a prize! ....

3 Where did they already get married? ....

4 He did built his house on the coast. ....

5 Where were you been an hour ago? ....

6 She has to chosen her wedding dress already. ....

5 ▸ **Complete the sentences with will or be going to.**

Ex.   *I'm really hungry. I think I .....will order..... a pizza. (order)*

1   I .... your pets while you are on vacation. (feed)

2   .... you .... any TV this evening? (watch)

3   What .... she .... Alice for her birthday? (buy)

4   You .... the movie, so don't go and see it. (not like)

5   .... I .... you with the housework? (help)

6   We .... to Dallas next month. (move)

7   Be careful! You .... the vase on the floor. (drop)

8   Don't eat in the library or the librarians .... you to leave. (ask)

6 ▸ **Choose the correct answer.**

Ex.   *Don't worry. You .... pass the test.*
   a *are going to*   **b** *are*   **c** *will*

1   .... I bring you something to drink?
   a Will   **b** Am   **c** Shall

2   Sue's making dinner for everyone .... evening.
   a today   **b** this   **c** in

3   I .... meeting Annie for dinner tonight.
   a am going to   **b** am   **c** will

4   We are leaving the house .... a minute.
   a in   **b** on   **c** at

5   When .... the plane leaving?
   a is going to   **b** will   **c** is

6   He will be fourteen years old .... year.
   a next   **b** other   **c** soon

7   .... you going to eat out tonight?
   a Will   **b** Are   **c** Shall

8   Bye, Sandra. I'll see you ....!
   a later   **b** next   **c** this day

7 ▸ **Find the mistakes and write the sentences correctly.**

Ex.   *She doesn't look very well. I think she will faint.*
   She doesn't look very well. I think she's going to faint.
....

1   Is that heavy? I'm going to carry it for you.
....

2   I will have a party on Saturday.
....

3   Look at those dark clouds! It will rain.
....

4   I think Jason is going lose his job.
....

5   I promise I'm going to help you.
....

6   No, I don't know the answer. I'm going to ask the teacher tomorrow.
....

7   Can you lend me your pen? I promise I'll to give it back.
....

8   Our friends will coming to stay next weekend.
....

8 ▶ **Choose the correct answer.**

Ex. He (could) / can *swim when he was two years old.*

1   *Can / Am able* I have some money for dinner?

2   She *was / can't* able to walk before she was one.

3   Tree frogs *could be / can* jump.

4   Will you *be able to / can* come home early from work?

5   Do you think he *could / will be able to* play chess well when he was a child?

6   No, you *aren't able to / can't* stay out until 1 o'clock in the morning!

7   *Could / Able* you bring me a glass of water, please?

8   He isn't *can / able to* come to school today.

9   We *can't / not able to* wait any longer.

10 *Am I able to / Can I* borrow the car tonight?

9 ▶ **Complete the sentences with can, could, was or will.**

Ex. She ....*was*............ not able to go to the party.

1   .... you be able to come to my house for dinner next week?

2   .... he read when he was three?

3   .... you lend me your black jeans, please?

4   When .... I leave the office today?

5   Look! .... you see that man? I think he's a famous actor.

6   When .... you be able to write back to me?

7   The flight was late and they .... not wait at the airport.

8   I don't think I .... finish the project on time. I need another week.

9   I tried very hard but I .... not able to understand the lesson.

10 .... I leave work early tomorrow?

10 ▶ **Find the extra word in each sentence and write it on the dotted line.**

Ex. *She couldn't to understand what he was saying.* ......*to*......

1   Could you to tell me where the post office is, please? ....

2   He is can play the guitar like a rock star. ....

3   Can you able play tennis on Saturday morning? ....

4   I can't not hear very well with my right ear. ....

5   We weren't able to not eat all the food we ordered. ....

6   She couldn't done sing well when she was a teenager. ....

7   Do you think they will to be able to come? ....

8   Can he able finish his work in time? ....

9   The cat was able to could climb down from the tree. ....

10 You can to go home at 6 o'clock. ....

11 ▶ Complete the sentences with **must, must not, has/have to** or **doesn't/don't have to.**

Ex. *You* .... *must not* .... *play loud music at night.*

1   You .... be careful when you carry the baby.
2   Laura .... iron the clothes because her husband does it.
3   Do you .... clean your room every day?
4   They .... be polite to their guests.
5   You .... be rude to your boss.
6   You .... make dinner tonight. We can order pizza.
7   You .... drive under the speed limit.
8   Melinda .... do any homework because she is only three.
9   We .... wear a jacket today. It's very hot.
10 She .... get up at 6 o'clock every morning.

12 ▶ Find the extra word in each sentence and write it on the dotted line.

Ex. *She will must leave the party early.* ...... *will* ......

1   We have to not get to the office by eight tomorrow. ....
2   You must to make notes on what the teacher says. ....
3   Did she have to have cook dinner when she was eleven? ....
4   Must I be say I'm sorry? ....
5   They don't have to must pay for the computer now. ....
6   Why does he do have to stay in tonight? ....
7   You must not be walk in the middle of the road. ....
8   You must to run every day so you can win the race. ....

13 ▶ Find the mistakes and write the sentences correctly.

Ex. *I must not finish my article before tomorrow.*
    I must finish my article before tomorrow.
    ....

1   I'll must to go to bed early tonight.
    ....

2   People not must waste water.
    ....

3   Do you have walk to the station?
    ....

4   You have visit the doctor regularly.
    ....

5   What time do she have to start work tomorrow?
    ....

6   We must not driving too fast.
    ....

7   You are have to work quietly in the library.
    ....

8   I don't must wash my clothes every day.
    ....

9 Relative Clauses

HE'S THE MAN WHO DOESN'T KNOW HOW TO MAKE COFFEE!

Relative Clauses

Relative clauses give us more information about the person, animal or thing we are talking about.

Relative clauses always begin with a relative pronoun like *who, that* or *which,* or a relative adverb like *where.*

Jenny is the girl who gave me this pen.
I've lost the key that opens my suitcase.
This is the college where I studied English.

We use:

➤ *who* or *that* for people.
 He's the man who/that hired me.

➤ *that* or *which* for animals or things.
 This is the house that/which my parents are buying.

➤ *where* for places.
 That's the town where I grew up.

---

1 ▸ **Complete the sentences with who/that, that/which or where.**

Ex. *Mary is the woman ......who/that...... gave the party.*

1 We're visiting the town .... our friend was born.

2 Is this the page .... fell out of your book?

3 Is that the man .... stole your pen?

4 The car .... is outside the house is my brother's.

5 That is the man .... is the manager of the other company.

6 I know a good restaurant .... we could go this evening.

7 Where's the money .... I left here?

8 Yesterday I met someone .... I haven't seen for years.

2 ▸ **Choose the correct answer.**

Ex. *I don't read books .... are very long.*
   a who   **b** where   **c** that ✓

1 Is that the house .... you lived ten years ago?
   a which   **b** where   **c** what

2 Those are the students .... got the best grades in English.
   a who   **b** what   **c** which

3 Is this the bakery .... they make great apple pies?
   a which   **b** who   **c** where

4 Have you seen the bag .... has my books in it?
   a which   **b** where   **c** what

5 That's the girl .... went to the movies with Richard.
   a what   **b** who   **c** where

6 This is the place .... I usually buy my clothes.
   a who   **b** which   **c** where

3 ▶ **Join the two sentences with** who, that, which **or** where. **More than one answer may be possible.**

Ex. *Gavin is a teenager. He crashed into my car.*
Gavin is the teenager who/that crashed into my car.

1   The Palace is a hotel. I work there.

   ....

2   This is a new CD. I just bought it.

   ....

3   John is a new student. He is studying math.

   ....

4   I play on the basketball team. It's the best team in town.

   ....

5   Mrs. Higgins is an old woman. She is a very good cook.

   ....

6   That's a fast food restaurant. We take our children there.

   ....

> **Think**about**it**
>
> When you join two sentences together using a relative pronoun or a relative adverb, don't include the subject or object pronoun that **who**, **that**, **which** or **where** is replacing.

4 ▶ **FInd the extra word in each sentence and write it on the dotted line.**

Ex. *Is he the boy for who went to your brother's school?* ...*for*...

1   She is where a good cook who always makes delicious meals. ....

2   Seattle is the city that it is famous for its Space Needle. ....

3   Have you visited the place where your father was born there? ....

4   Are those the boots that Daniel who gave you? ....

5   Is she the woman to who you met in town yesterday? ....

6   I couldn't find the shop where you can buy which cheap jeans. ....

7   Kevin is the man who he lives next door. ....

8   The girl who she helped me is over there. ....

5 ▶ **Match.**

Ex. *That old factory is*

1   My brother is

2   That's the

3   She is the doctor

4   Those are the roses

5   That's the man who

6   Have you seen the place where

a   hospital where I was born.

b   the person who rescued the cat from the river.

c   that we planted last year.

d   gave us our dog.

e   *where we worked years ago.*

f   they make jewelry?

g   who helped my sister.

6 ▷ **Write the words in the correct order.**

Ex. *eyes / has / he / boy / green / the / is / who / .*
     He is the boy who has green eyes.
     ....

1 you / is / where / the / lived / place / this / ?
   ....

2 Ann / golf / who / is / the / plays / girl / .
   ....

3 all / that / have / sleeps / we / cat / a / day / .
   ....

4 the / that / car / is / you / saw / which / ?
   ....

5 house / the / where / that's / John/ lives / .
   ....

6 I / tall / man / feet / who / six / is / met / a / .
   ....

7 ▷ **Find the mistakes and write the sentences correctly. More than one answer may be possible.**

Ex. *The man over there is the person which taught me how to swim.*
     The man over there is the person who/that taught me how to swim.
     ....

1 The house what they have bought is near the beach.
   ....

2 This is the dog who I found in the street.
   ....

3 The man who is singing he is my friend.
   ....

4 We met a person yesterday was very polite.
   ....

5 Can I see where the laptop that your wife bought you?
   ....

6 This is the park which I first played baseball.
   ....

8 ▷ **Complete the sentences with who, that, which or where and the phrases from the box.**

---
make bread and cakes   wrote many famous plays   lots of people work   travel in space   live on farms
is close to Mexico   we learn interesting things   came from South America   every student needs
---

Ex. *Astronauts are people* ..*who/that travel in space.*..

1 Cows are animals ....
2 School is the place ....
3 El Paso is a city ....
4 Shakespeare is an author ....
5 Factories are buildings ....
6 Bakers are people ....
7 A dictionary is a book ....
8 Tomatoes are a fruit ....

9   **Complete the sentences in your own words.**

Ex.   *I know a man who* ....*owns four cars.*...

1   I don't know anybody who ....

2   I like to read books that ....

3   I like people who ....

4   I went on vacation to a place where ....

5   I've never been to a city where ....

Pairwork

Work with a partner. Take turns. Tell your partner about two people that you know, two places that you have visited and two movies that you have seen. Use relative clauses.

Writing

Write a paragraph about your family and home. Use relative clauses to describe your family, the things in your house and the neighborhood where you live.

10 Nouns & Articles

HE WANTED TO BUY ME A CUP OF COFFEE BUT HE DIDN'T HAVE ANY MONEY

Plural Nouns

Regular Plurals

We usually make a noun plural by adding *-s*.

| girl | ➜ | girls |
| cat | ➜ | cats |

When a noun ends in *-s, -ss, -sh, -ch, -x* or *-o*, we add *-es*.

bus	➜	buses	watch	➜	watches
kiss	➜	kisses	fox	➜	foxes
brush	➜	brushes	potato	➜	potatoes

When a noun ends in a consonant and *-y*, we take off the *-y* and add *-ies*.

| baby | ➜ | babies |
| lady | ➜ | ladies |

When a noun ends in a vowel and *-y*, we add *-s*.

| boy | ➜ | boys |
| donkey | ➜ | donkeys |

When a noun ends in *-f* or *-fe*, we usually add *-ves*.

| leaf | ➜ | leaves | | roof | ➜ | roofs |
| wife | ➜ | wives | BUT | giraffe | ➜ | giraffes |

Irregular Plurals

Some nouns are irregular. We make them plural in different ways.

child	➜	children
fish	➜	fish
foot	➜	feet
man	➜	men
mouse	➜	mice
sheep	➜	sheep
tooth	➜	teeth
woman	➜	women

Notes

We do not use *a* or *an* before a plural noun.
This is a newspaper.
These are newspapers.

---

1 ▶ Change the singular nouns to plural nouns. Make other changes as needed.

Ex. *The car is new.*
The cars are new.
....

1 The butterfly is on the leaf.

....

2 The mouse has a long tail.

....

3 The watch is broken.

....

4 The baby is crying.

....

5 Put the ball in the box.

....

6 The red dress is beautiful.

....

Count and Noncount Nouns

Count Nouns

Most nouns are count nouns, and they have a plural form.

bird	➜	birds
sandwich	➜	sandwiches
mouse	➜	mice

Don't forget that we do not use *a* or *an* with plural nouns. We can use the word *some* with plural nouns in affirmative sentences. We can use the word *any* with plural nouns in negative sentences and in questions.

She has a book. ➜	She has some books.
He doesn't have a brother. ➜	He doesn't have any brothers.
Did you bring a book to read? ➜	Did you bring any books to read?

Noncount Nouns

Some nouns are noncount nouns and do not have a plural form.

bread	lemonade
cheese	luggage
chocolate	meat
furniture	money
hair	water

We do not use *a* or *an* with noncount nouns. We can use the word *some* in affirmative sentences. We can use the word *any* in negative sentences and questions.

I want some cheese.
He has some bread and juice.
They don't have any money.
Is there any meat in the freezer?

When we are offering something to someone, we often use the word *some*. We do not use the word *any*.

Do you want some juice?
Would you like some chocolate?

We can use the following words to talk about quantities of noncount nouns.

bread	➜	a loaf of bread	two loaves of bread
soda	➜	a can of soda	two cans of soda
lemonade	➜	a glass of lemonade	two glasses of lemonade
milk	➜	a carton of milk	two cartons of milk
rice	➜	a bowl of rice	two bowls of rice
soup	➜	a can of soup	two cans of soup
coffee	➜	a cup of coffee	two cups of coffee
water	➜	a bottle of water	two bottles of water

---

2 ▶ **Write C for count nouns and N for noncount nouns and write the plural if there is one.**

	Noun	C or N	Plural
Ex.	*tomato*	*C*	*tomatoes*
	sugar	*N*	*–*
1	egg		
2	water		
3	air		
4	sandwich		
5	advice		
6	honey		
7	cherry		
8	information		
9	money		
10	dollar		

3 ▶ **Complete the sentences with some or any.**

Ex. *Do you have .....any..... chocolate?*

1 I want .... bread and butter, please.

2 There isn't .... rice left.

3 We don't have .... eggs.

4 Would you like .... coffee?

5 Do you have .... lemonade?

6 There isn't .... sugar in the cupboard.

7 I don't want .... salt, thanks.

8 There are .... cookies on the table.

Articles

The Indefinite Article *a* / *an*
We use the indefinite article:

➤ with singular count nouns.
I saw a lizard.
He rides an elephant in the circus.

➤ when we are not talking about something specific.
I need a pen. (any pen)
Do you have a coat? (any coat)

➤ before an adjective before a singular count noun.
That's an interesting book.
He owns a black horse.

➤ to talk about people's jobs.
She's an airline pilot.

Notes

When a word begins with a vowel that sounds like a consonant in the word, we use *a*.
Annie goes to a university in California.
The soldier is wearing a uniform.

When a word begins with a consonant that sounds like a vowel in the word, we use *an*.
This shop will close in an hour.
My aunt is an honest woman.

---

4 ▶ **Complete the sentences with a, an or –.**

Ex.   *They have* ....*a*.... *new car.*

1   Would you like .... orange?
2   He is .... professor at .... university in Boston.
3   Don't forget to buy .... milk.
4   I bought .... new skirt yesterday.
5   I want to get .... dog.
6   She's got .... lovely hair.

Articles

The Definite Article *the*
We use the definite article:

➤ with singular and plural count nouns and with noncount nouns.
The window is broken.
The windows are broken.
The tea is cold.

➤ when we are talking about something specific.
The flowers that you bought are on the table.

➤ when we are talking about something that is unique.
The Statue of Liberty is in New York.
The sun is shining today.

➤ before the superlative form of adjectives and adverbs.
She is the youngest student in the class.
That's the fastest I've ever run!

➤ with musical instruments.
I play the piano.
Do you play the drums?

➤ with the names of seas (*the Mediterranean*), rivers (*the East River*), oceans (*the Pacific Ocean*), deserts (*the Sahara Desert*), mountain ranges (*the Alps*), groups of islands (*the Galapagos Islands*), some countries (*the United States of America*), hotels (*the Hilton Hotel*), theaters (*the Lowes Theater*) and newspapers (*The Times*).

We do not use the definite article or the indefinite article with:

➤ plural nouns when we are talking in general.
Children love sweets.
People enjoy having barbecues.

➤ people's names.
I see Ruth every day.

➤ names of streets, avenues and roads.
They live on Bridge Street.

➤ names of towns and cities.
He's going to London next week.

➤ names of islands.
Have you ever been to Hawaii?

➤ names of continents and most countries.
We went to Australia last year.

➤ names of meals.
I have breakfast at 8 o'clock.

➤ nouns that describe abstract things.
Beauty is not as important as kindness.

➤ the words *home, work, school, prison* and *bed* in phrases that refer to a place generally.
Why are you in bed? You should be at work!

5 ▶ Complete the sentences with **the** or **–** .

Ex. *My grandmother is in ...the... hospital at the moment.*

1 The Brooklyn Bridge is in .... New York.

2 Let's stay at .... Ambassador Hotel.

3 Do you like .... animals?

4 Who is .... oldest person you know?

5 What time are we having .... lunch?

6 Let's go and look at .... sun setting over the sea.

7 They liked .... present which I bought them.

8 Have you seen .... Judy?

6 ▶ Complete the sentences with **a, an, the** or **–** .

Ex. *There is ....a.... swimming competition on Saturday.*

1 The burglar has been in .... prison since June.

2 I didn't know you were .... newspaper reporter.

3 Look at .... apples on that tree!

4 Do you usually go to .... bed at 11 o'clock?

5 I think .... patience is a good quality to have.

6 He's always wanted to visit .... United States.

7 He's .... very intelligent person.

8 I'd like .... cup of tea, please.

7 ▶ Find the mistakes and write the sentences correctly.

Ex. *He is artist who paints portraits of famous people.*
  He is an artist who paints portraits of famous people.

1 Let's buy any bread and cheese and go on a picnic.
  ....

2 I love practicing a piano every day.
  ....

3 I'd love any soup.
  ....

4 It's fun to swim in an ocean.
  ....

5 There are two carton of milks in the refrigerator.
  ....

6 Don't forget to buy two breads.
  ....

8 ▶ Choose the correct answer.

Ex. *Are you .... man who repairs computers?*
  a *any*   **(b)** *the*   **c** *one*

1 My father is .... police officer in Atlanta.
  a the   **b** –   **c** a

2 Have you ever been to .... Hawaii?
  a the   **b** –   **c** an

3 George Washington was .... first president of the United States.
  a the   **b** a   **c** some

4 They're going on a cruise around .... world.
  a a   **b** any   **c** the

5 Have you met .... people who live next door?
  a –   **b** a   **c** the

6 Do we have .... soap?
  a any   **b** some   **c** a

7 There isn't .... furniture in our new house yet.
  a some   **b** the   **c** any

8 Where are .... Rocky Mountains?
  a some   **b** the   **c** any

9 ► **Complete the sentences with your own ideas. Use a, an, the, some, any and – at least once in your sentences.**

Ex.   Egypt is .... *an interesting country* ....

1   Let's buy Mom .... for her birthday.

2   I've never seen ....

3   Where are .... that I left on my desk?

4   Do you want to go to .... with me?

5   Is there .... for dinner?

6   I usually have .... for breakfast.

7   That new movie is .... I've ever seen.

8   I'd like to go to .... next year.

Pairwork

Work with a partner. Tell each other about a trip or vacation you went on.
Think about:
➤ where you went.   ➤ how you got there.
➤ what sights you saw.   ➤ what you did there.
➤ what you ate and drank.   ➤ what time you got home.

Writing

Write about a place you know well. Think about:
➤ where it is.
➤ what's special about it.
➤ what sights there are.
➤ what activities you can do there.
➤ why you like it or don't like it.

....
....
....
....
....
....
....
....
....
....
....
....
....
....
....
....
....

THERE'S TOO MUCH WORK AND NOT ENOUGH TIME!

A Little, A Few, A Lot Of

We use *a little* with noncount nouns. It means "not much."
There's a little water left in the bottle.

We use *a few* and *a few of* with count nouns. They both mean "not many."
There are a few children in the park.
A few of my friends went on vacation together.

We use *a lot of* with noncount nouns and with plural count nouns.
It means "much/many." We usually use it in an affirmative sentence.
We've got a lot of information to read.
There are a lot of students in my math class.

Notes

The phrase *lots of* is an informal form of *a lot of*. The meaning is the same. We can use it with both noncount and plural count nouns.
We had lots of fun yesterday.
There were lots of people at the party.

---

1 ▷ **Complete the sentences with a few or a little.**

Ex. *We only have* ....*a little*.... *time before the guests arrive.*

1 I'm going shopping. There are .... things I need.

2 .... of my friends are going to the movies tonight.

3 I just got this apartment, so I only have .... furniture.

4 There are .... eggs in the refrigerator.

5 My father only puts .... salt in his soup.

6 I knew .... of the people at the party, but not many.

7 We saw .... swans on the pond when we were walking in the park yesterday.

8 I wasn't very thirsty, so I only drank .... water.

2 ▶ Choose the correct answer.

Ex.   I need .... sugar for this recipe.

a a few   **ⓑ** a lot of   **c** little of

1   I have .... books about the environment at home.

a a little   **b** a lot   **c** a few

2   There were .... people at the concert last night.

a a little of   **b** a lot of   **c** little

3   There is .... bread left.

a a little   **b** a few   **c** a lot

4   Would you like .... strawberries with your ice cream?

a a few   **b** a little   **c** lot of

Thinkaboutit

We use **a little** for noncount nouns and **a few** for count nouns. We can use **a lot of** to talk about both count and noncount nouns.

5   Can I have .... butter for my bread, please?

a a few   **b** a little   **c** a lot

6   There are only .... eggs left.

a an   **b** a few   **c** a lot of

Much, Many

We use *much* with noncount nouns in negative sentences and questions.
There isn't much bread in the bag.
Is there much coffee left?

We use *many* with plural count nouns.
We usually use it in negative sentences and questions.
There aren't many young children in my family.
Are there many stores in your neighborhood?

3 ▶ Complete the sentences with much or many.

Ex.   I haven't seen .....*many*..... tourists so far this year.

1   He doesn't want .... people to come to his party.

2   She doesn't put .... salt on her food.

3   Do you have .... CDs in your collection?

4   Do you know .... students who are studying chemistry?

5   We don't have .... money, but we're happy.

6   There isn't .... time, so you must hurry.

Both, Either, Neither

We use *both*, *neither* and *either* to talk about two people, two animals or two things.

Both ... and ... / Both of ...
Both means "one and the other." We always use *both* with a plural affirmative verb.
Both Sarah and Kate are coming for dinner.
Both of the girls live near me.

Either ... or ... / Either of ...
Either means "one or the other." We usually use *either of ...* in negative statements and questions.
Either John or Suzie has a birthday today. I forget who.
I don't like either spinach or mushrooms.

Have you seen either of the twins today?
No, I haven't seen either of them.

Neither ... nor / Neither of ...
Neither means "not one or the other." We always use *neither* with an affirmative verb, but the meaning is negative.
Neither Tim nor Dave has ever been to Japan.
Neither my parents nor my friends have ever been to Mexico.
Neither of the two boys has ever traveled by plane.

4 ▶ **Complete the sentences with both, either or neither.**

Ex.   *I don't like ......either...... beef or lamb.*

1   Can you believe that .... Tom nor David has ever used a computer?

2   The library doesn't have .... of the books I want.

3   "Which dress should I buy?"

     "................ the blue one or the black one. .... of them look good on you."

4   I love geography and history. .... subjects interest me very much.

5   .... of the twins is good at geography.

6   I'm thinking of studying .... computers or business.

7   .... Tom and Ben take piano lessons.

8   .... of those coats fits you. Don't buy .... of them.

All / All of, None of

We use *all* and *none of* to talk about more than two people, animals or things.

All / All of ...
All and *all of* mean "every one of (a group)." When used as the subject, they are followed by a verb in the third person plural.
All children have the right to a good education.
All of the employees are here today. = All the employees are here today.
She asked all of us to the party.

None of ...
None of means "not even one of." In American English we usually use it with a singular affirmative verb.
None of us on the staff is going on vacation this month because we're very busy.
None of my friends likes spinach.

5 ▶ **Choose the correct answer.**

Ex.   (All) / None *of my friends have read the Harry Potter books. We loved them!*

1   We have two old cassette players at home and *neither / none* of them is working.

2   *All / None* of my parents' friends has ever been to Japan, but a few of them are planning to go next year.

3   My tennis coach has three sons, and *both / all* of them are excellent athletes.

4   *All / None* of the students heard the teacher because they weren't paying attention.

5   I read *none / both* of the books he gave me. I just haven't had time lately.

Too Much, Too Many

We use *too much* and *too many* to talk about a quantity that is bigger than we want or need.

Too much + noncount noun
There's too much salt in this soup.

Too many + plural count noun
There are too many people on this bus!

6 ▶ Complete the sentences with **too much** or **too many**.

Ex. *Is there* ......*too much*...... *butter on the bread?*

1 He gave me .... money for the taxi, so I gave him some back.

2 I think there are .... people on the bus. It's not safe.

3 I have .... work to do. I'll never finish it today!

4 There are .... things for me to do today. I'll ask Ann to help me.

5 Do you think there are .... cars on the roads these days?

6 You can never have .... free time!

Not Enough

We use *not enough* to talk about a quantity that is smaller than we want or need.

Not enough + noncount noun or count noun
There's not enough sugar in my coffee.
There aren't enough chairs for everyone.

7 ▶ Complete the sentences with **too much, too many** or **not enough**.

Ex. *There are* ....*not enough*............... *chairs for everyone, so some people will have to stand.*

1 I believe there's .... litter on the streets. It's bad for the environment.

2 There are .... things for young people to do in my town, so they get bored.

3 I can't go out tonight. I have .... work to do.

4 I've eaten .... french fries and now I feel sick!

5 There's .... water in the dog's bowl. He needs more.

6 Don't give that little boy .... chocolate to eat.

7 There are .... factories in this city. The pollution is terrible.

8 There is .... cake for everyone. I'll buy more.

8 ▶ Choose the correct answer.

Ex. *There were* too much / a few *people at the concert last Saturday.*

1 We don't have *enough / none* money to buy that laptop.

2 *None / Too many* of the students understood the teacher's explanation.

3 I can't give you *enough / much* help. I have to leave soon.

4 Moving costs *too many / too much* money. I prefer to stay here.

5 *All / Either* the people I know love to travel.

6 I need *none / a little* cheese for my pizza.

7 Could you give me *too much / a little* rice, please?

8 There is *not enough / too much* coffee. Please make some more.

9 ▶ **Find the mistakes and write the sentences correctly.**

Ex. *There are too much people in this city.*
    There are too many people in this city. ....

1   I'm only taking a few luggage with me on vacation.
    ....

2   Neither of the people in my town wanted a new highway.
    ....

3   There are enough trees in the park. We must plant more.
    ....

4   Either my brother nor my sister lives at home.
    ....

5   Neither Jill and Ann love soap operas. They watch them every day!
    ....

6   There's too many noise coming from next door again.
    ....

7   Do you know none of the students in your class?
    ....

8   There are a little sandwiches and some soda left for lunch.
    ....

10 ▶ **Complete the sentences with the words from the box.**

| all   both   either   lot of   much   neither   not enough |

Ex. *There are ......not enough...... people in our office. They need to hire more.*

1   I don't eat a .... fish, but I know it's good for you.
2   Some people think movie stars earn too .... money.
3   She has .... the books by that author.
4   .... my brothers live in Florida.
5   .... of my parents has ever been to Europe.
6   We can go to .... the Italian restaurant or the Thai restaurant. I'll let you decide.

11 ▶ **Match.**

Ex. *He can speak a lot*   a   money?
1   They don't have many   b   all your money?
2   Does he have much   c   *of languages.*
3   There aren't enough stamps   d   studying languages?
4   Are they both   e   milk left.
5   There's only a little   f   friends.
6   Have you spent   g   for all the letters.

12 ▶ **Choose the correct answer.**

Ex. *There are too .... things to carry.*
    a *much*   **b** *enough*   ⓒ *many*

1   Can I have a .... sugar for my coffee, please?
    a few   **b** little   **c** lot

2   .... of my friends likes opera.
    a Either   **b** Both   **c** None

3   There is .... time to do everything!
    a too many   **b** not enough   **c** a few

4   I haven't done .... housework this week.
    a many   **b** not enough   **c** much

5   We can watch .... of these two movies.
    a neither   **b** none   **c** either

6   .... people care about the environment.
    a Too much   **b** Not enough   **c** None

7   I need .... fruit for this recipe.
    a a lot of   **b** too many   **c** both

8   There are holes in .... my shoes.
    a either   **b** both   **c** neither

Pairwork

Work with a partner. Take turns. Ask and answer questions about what you usually eat. Use the words you have studied in this unit. For example: Do you eat a lot of fish? Do you like both apples and oranges?

Writing

Think about the questions you asked above. Write a paragraph about the food you and the people in your family eat. Use the words you have studied in this unit.

I HAD FINISHED ALL MY WORK BY 2 O'CLOCK, SO I TOLD THE BOSS, AND HE FOUND SOMETHING ELSE FOR ME TO DO!

Past Perfect

Affirmative	Negative	Question
I had (I'd) stopped	I had not (hadn't) stopped	Had I stopped?
you had (you'd) stopped	you had not (hadn't) stopped	Had you stopped?
he had (he'd) stopped	he had not (hadn't) stopped	Had he stopped?
she had (she'd) stopped	she had not (hadn't) stopped	Had she stopped?
it had (it'd) stopped	it had not (hadn't) stopped	Had it stopped?
we had (we'd) stopped	we had not (hadn't) stopped	Had we stopped?
you had (you'd) stopped	you had not (hadn't) stopped	Had you stopped?
they had (they'd) stopped	they had not (hadn't) stopped	Had they stopped?

Short Answers

Yes, I/you had.	No, I/you hadn't.
Yes, he/she/it had.	No, he/she/it hadn't.
Yes, we/you/they had.	No, we/you/they hadn't.

We form the Past Perfect with *had* and the past participle of the main verb. See the Irregular Verbs list on page 132.

We use the Past Perfect to talk about:

➤ something that happened in the past before another action in the past. For the action that happened first, we use the Past Perfect. For the later action, we use the Simple Past.
I called her at 8 a.m. but she had already left for work.

➤ something that happened before a specific time in the past.
He had had his meeting by 3 o'clock.

➤ something that happened in the past that had an effect on a following action or state.
I had left my umbrella at home, so I got soaking wet when it started to rain.

---

1 ▶ **Write SP if the verb is in the Simple Past and PP if the verb is in the Past Perfect.**

Ex. *He went to school and studied hard.* ___SP___

1 He had studied hard before the test. _____
2 By the end of July he had read five books. _____
3 We watched a basketball game last Saturday. _____
4 Before last year I had never seen a Manx cat. _____
5 They came to the party and danced all night. _____
6 By 1970 astronauts had walked on the moon. _____
7 Had he eaten the sandwiches by 12 o'clock? _____
8 She had a shower this morning. _____

2 ▶ **Complete the sentences with the Past Perfect.**

Ex. *They ....had finished.......... their dinner before I called. (finish)*

1   I .... to Mark in months, so I decided to call him. (speak)

2   Everybody .... home by midnight. (go)

3   By 9 o'clock they still .... breakfast. (not have)

4   She .... some great food for the party. (make)

5   I .... my new jacket by last week. (buy)

6   They .... what to buy before they went shopping. (not decide)

3 ▶ **Write questions and negative sentences.**

Ex. *She had washed her hair before the party.*

Had she washed her hair before the party?

She hadn't washed her hair before the party.

1   He had fallen asleep by 2 o'clock.

....

....

2   He had forgotten to buy Rachel a present.

....

....

3   She had eaten too much.

....

....

4   The artist had sold ten paintings by December.

....

....

5   They had cleaned the kitchen by lunchtime.

....

....

6   He had cooked dinner before the game started.

....

....

4 ▶ **Complete the sentences with the Past Perfect. Use the verbs from the box.**

| ask | begin | do | eat | go | pass | send | stay | win |

Ex. *He was tired because he .....had stayed.... up late the night before.*

1   I came to see you yesterday but you .... out.

2   I called Dana to invite her to the party but Rosa .... her already.

3   By the time we arrived at the theater, the play .... already ....

4   Jenny asked me to iron her skirt but I .... it already.

5   The fans were excited because their team .... the game.

6   I .... you several e-mails by the time your letter finally arrived.

7   I .... a late lunch, so I wasn't hungry when I got home.

8   She was happy because she .... all her courses.

Time Expressions

after	by (a time or date)
already	just
before	

After she had packed her bags, she went to the airport.
I tried to call you, but you had already left.
He had looked at dozens of TVs before he made his final decision.
By May I had moved to a new house.
When I arrived, the movie had just started.

---

5 ▶ **Complete the sentences with the Simple Past or the Past Perfect.**

Ex. He .... *was* .... very thirsty because he .... *hadn't had* .... any water. (be, not have)

1 The teacher .... at her because she ....
her homework. (shout, not do)

2 Jane .... happy because her husband ....
to buy her a birthday present. (feel, remember)

3 The famous mystery writer .... over a hundred novels by
the time she .... (write, die)

4 The burglar .... by the time the police ....
(escape, arrive)

5 The store .... by the time we .... there.
(already close, get)

6 He .... at many cars before he .... on the
one he wanted. (not look, decide)

7 He .... a car after he .... enough money. (buy, save)

8 I .... already .... the cake before she .... home. (make, get)

> **Thinkaboutit**
>
> When there are two actions in the past, always think about which action happened first. That is the action we put into the Past Perfect.

---

6 ▶ **Find the mistakes and write the sentences correctly.**

Ex. *Vincent had left home before I had got up this morning.*
Vincent had left home before I got up this morning.

1 She eaten all the ice cream and didn't leave any for me!
....

2 Have you been to the USA before your vacation in New York last year?
....

3 I read the book by the time the class started.
....

4 We never saw a real lion before we went to the zoo.
....

5 When I saw her, she already been to the dentist.
....

6 When I leave the house, it had already started to rain.
....

7 I already washed the car before I went to work.
....

8 My brother had received my postcard after I had returned.
....

7 ▷ **Combine each group of sentences. Use the words in parentheses.**

Ex. *My son went out at 7 o'clock. I got home at 8 o'clock. (before)*
     My son had gone out before I got home...

1   I ate too much. I felt sick. (so)

     ....

2   The police arrived at 2 o'clock. The accident happened at 1 o'clock. (after)

     ....

3   Helen fed the cat at 7 o'clock. She went to bed at 12 o'clock. (before)

     ....

4   He went to work at 8 o'clock. He washed the car at 7 o'clock. (after)

     ....

5   She finished the report. Then she went to the meeting. (before)

     ....

6   He slept for an hour. He felt much better. (after)

     ....

7   The children were happy. It snowed all night. (because)

     ....

8   I forgot my bag. I went back home. (so)

     ....

8 ▷ **Match.**

Ex. *After the alarm had rung,*   a   before I took a shower.
1   I had finished my report,   b   a week before she had her birthday party.
2   I had played tennis   c   *we went back to sleep.*
3   I'd already read the book, so   d   so I went to the beach with my friend.
4   We had bought Melissa's present   e   I didn't want to see the movie.
5   I surfed the Internet   f   before I passed my driving test.
6   I'd taken twenty lessons   g   after I'd sent my e-mails.

9 ▶ **Complete the sentences in your own words. Use the Past Perfect.**

Ex.   *By 9 o'clock this morning* ....*I had already eaten breakfast.*..

1   Before I got home, ...

2   Before I went to bed last night, ...

3   My friend was sad because ....

4   We all felt cold because ....

5   After I had gone out yesterday, ...

6   After I had eaten my dinner last night, ...

7   I'd left my keys at home, so ....

8   By last week ....

Pairwork

Work with a partner. Take turns. Ask and answer questions about last weekend. Use time expressions with sentences in the Simple Past and Past Perfect. Here is an example:

A: What did you do on Saturday afternoon?
B: I washed my car.
A: Before you washed your car, had you done anything else?
B: Sure. After I'd eaten breakfast, I called my friend Liz and we went to the mall. I'd seen a great pair of jeans in Fun Fashions the week before, so we ....

Writing

Make a list of things you did last weekend. Then write a paragraph about your weekend. Include sentences with the Past Perfect, the Simple Present and the time expressions from this unit.

1 ▶ **Choose the correct answer or answers. (NOTE: In two questions, both answers are correct.)**

Ex. *This is the photograph* (that)/ *who he showed me.*

1 He's the man *who / which* helped me.

2 I liked the book *who / that* you lent me last week.

3 That's the road *that / which* leads to my office.

4 Are you the sports expert *that / which* knows all about the history of baseball?

5 Is this the dog *which / who* belongs to Ellen?

6 English is the only subject *who / that* I enjoy.

7 Is this the boy *that / who* hit you?

8 Were you on the bus *which / who* was two hours late?

2 ▶ **Complete the sentences with that or where.**

Ex. *Where is the pen* .....*that*..... *I was using?*

1 That's the factory .... John works as a manager.

2 He lives in a town .... there are no trees.

3 Is this the bag .... you lost last week?

4 Have you seen the movie .... is about teenage rock stars?

5 Is that the shop .... you used to work?

6 Isn't that the hospital .... you were born?

7 I live in an area .... is polluted.

8 This is the place .... it happened.

3 ▶ **Find the extra word in each sentence and write it on the dotted line.**

Ex. *This is the girl who I was telling you about her.* ....*her*....

1 Do you know who the restaurant where we're going tonight? ....

2 Is Darren the person who knows all about which cooking? ....

3 These are the clothes that David who bought me. ....

4 Have you been to a which place where they sell furniture? ....

5 Where are the children who they are going to school? ....

6 This isn't the food which we who ordered! ....

7 Is there a bakery in the area where I can buy which good bread? ....

8 Look! There's a place where there we can have a picnic. ....

4 ▶ **Choose the correct answer.**

Ex. *Where are the earrings* .... *I gave you last week?*
    (a) *that*   b *who*   c *what*

1 There's a great restaurant in town .... you can buy cheap pizzas.
    a which   b where   c who

2 The woman with the big hat is the one .... hates dogs.
    a which   b what   c who

3 The man with Sally is the man .... she's going to marry.
    a what   b who   c which

4 Take me somewhere .... it's quiet and relaxing.
    a where   b which   c who

5 Is that the house .... you used to live?
    a which   b where   c what

6 I don't know the actor .... is starring in this movie.
    a who   b which   c who he

5 ▶ **Complete the sentences with the plural form of the noun.**

Ex.   *She gave the baby lots of ....kisses.......... . (kiss)*

1   They sell fantastic .... in that store. (book)

2   We waited for two hours, and then two .... came at once. (bus)

3   You can't buy those shoes! Your .... are too big! (foot)

4   How many .... did you use in this recipe? (potato)

5   How many .... have applied for the job? (woman)

6   Are you scared of ....? (mouse)

7   Husbands and .... are welcome at the office party. (wife)

8   Let's put all the shoes back in the .... (box)

9   Put the .... away when you have finished your painting. (brush)

10   The dentist removed two of her .... (tooth)

6 ▶ **Look at the underlined nouns and write C for count noun or N for noncount noun.**

Ex.   *There were two <u>kittens</u> on the bed.   __C__*

1   Let's have a <u>sandwich</u> for lunch. _____

2   Is there any <u>milk</u> in the fridge? _____

3   My grandfather grows his own <u>tomatoes</u>. _____

4   You usually eat <u>rice</u> with Indian food. _____

5   Do you prefer tea or <u>coffee</u>? _____

6   How do bees make <u>honey</u>? _____

7   I'm going to buy a <u>bottle</u> of water. _____

8   Can I have the <u>cherry</u> off the top of your ice cream sundae? _____

7 ▶ **Complete the sentences with some or any.**

Ex.   *Would you like ....some.... orange juice?*

1   There's .... milk in the carton.

2   I don't want .... butter on my bread, thanks.

3   They bought .... new furniture last weekend.

4   Are there .... cherries in the bowl?

5   Can I get you .... coffee?

6   I don't want .... chocolate. I'm on a diet.

7   Do you want .... coffee?

8   You can't take .... luggage with you in the helicopter.

8 ▶ **Complete the sentences with a, an, the or –.**

Ex.   *Where is ...the... cake I bought?*

1   I didn't know your brother was .... driving instructor.

2   You must not look right at .... sun.

3   Have you ever seen .... elephants in the wild?

4   We watched .... interesting documentary on TV last night.

5   What time shall we have .... lunch?

6   I haven't been to .... concert in years.

7   I'm so glad I live in .... Chicago.

8   It's time to put .... baby to bed.

9   Have you ever skied in .... Rocky Mountains?

10   I can't afford to stay at .... hotel near the lake.

9 ▸ Choose the correct answer.

Ex. *We've only got* ⟨a little⟩/ *a lot of money left.*

1 Do you eat *a lot of / a few* sugar every day?

2 There's only *a lot of / a little* cheese left, so don't use it all.

3 There are *a few / a little* eggs in the bird's nest.

4 *A few of / A little of* my friends are coming to my house tonight.

5 There isn't *a few of / a lot of* milk left.

6 I left *a few / a little* things at your house.

7 *A lot of / A few of* people think that he is a liar.

8 I only want *a lot of / a little* milk in my coffee, please.

10 ▸ Complete the sentences with **much** or **many**.

Ex. *You haven't eaten* ....*much*.... *food.*

1 Have you visited .... different places?

2 How .... new furniture will they need when they move?

3 How .... times have I told you not to do that!

4 I don't know .... people who can speak more than two languages.

5 Do you know if there is .... salt in this soup?

6 We must hurry! There isn't .... time.

7 I don't think there are .... turtles in this area.

8 There isn't .... pollution in the area where I live.

11 ▸ Complete the sentences with the words from the box.

both (x2)   neither   all (x2)   either (x2)   none of (x2)

Ex. ....*Both*........ *history and geography are easy subjects for me.*

1 I don't like .... of these books very much.

2 I've asked all my friends, but .... them wants to come with me.

3 .... Naomi and Christy will help you clean the house.

4 .... Gary or Emily will help you wash the car.

5 The students dislike homework, but they .... like sports.

6 .... the desserts on the menu was very expensive.

7 .... of the two girls understands the question.

8 .... of those people live in my building. They're my neighbors.

12 ▸ Complete the sentences with **too much, too many** or **not enough**.

Ex. *There were* ......*too many*...... *people at the party, so we ran out of food.*

1 Do you think young people spend .... time playing computer games?

2 There are .... chairs for all the guests to sit on. A few of us will have to stand.

3 It's not a good idea to eat .... food. You'll get sick.

4 "Shall we make some ice cream?" "No, there's .... milk."

5 You put .... salt in the soup. It tastes awful!

6 Don't let the children eat .... cookies.

7 I can't finish the report because there is .... time.

8 There were .... people in in the ticket line, so we went home.

13 ▶ **Complete the sentences with the Past Perfect.**

Ex.   *Before last year I* ....*had never traveled*........... *around the USA. (never travel)*

1   They .... each other for three years before they got married. (know)

2   She .... the play before. (see)

3   Where .... you .... before you moved here? (live)

4   He felt tired because he .... up very late the night before. (stay)

5   I was surprised to see that it .... during the night. (snow)

6   She .... about it very carefully before she decided. (not think)

7   .... they .... of sleeping sickness before they went to Africa? (hear)

8   After he .... about it, he realized she was right. (think)

14 ▶ **Complete the sentences with the Simple Past or the Past Perfect.**

Ex.   *She* ....*had made*.... *the dinner by the time I* ....*got*.......... *there. (make, get)*

1   He .... sick because he .... too much chocolate cake. (be, eat)

2   We .... lots of houses by the time we .... this one. (see, choose)

3   I .... to the concert because I .... my ticket. (not go, lose)

4   He .... his driver's test after he .... it three times! (pass, take)

5   Joe .... sad because he .... his dog. (be, lose)

6   By the time I .... to the theater, the play .... (get, start)

7   .... he .... any driving lessons before he .... a car? (have, buy)

8   I .... my work by the time Gary .... home. (finish, get)

15 ▶ **Choose the correct answer.**

Ex.   *The mail carrier* .... *left before I opened the door.*
   a *has*   **ⓑ** *had*   **c** *is*

1   I called to see you, but you had .... out.
   a go   **b** went   **c** gone

2   I wanted to watch the movie on TV, but my friends .... seen it.
   a has already   **b** had already   **c** already had

3   He .... very excited because he had won the competition.
   a had been   **b** had being   **c** was

4   We couldn't go out until the rain ....
   a has stopped   **b** stops   **c** had stopped

5   I saw the movie .... I had read the book.
   a before   **b** after   **c** by

6   By June the flowers ....
   a has bloomed   **b** have bloomed   **c** had bloomed

7   The beach .... dirty because there had been a storm.
   a is   **b** had been   **c** was

8   .... I got there, the meeting had already started.
   a By the time   **b** After   **c** By 6 o'clock

YOU PARKED IN THE DIRECTOR'S PARKING SPOT AGAIN, DIDN'T YOU?

Tag Questions

She is an actress, isn't she?
You speak German, don't you?
They are doing the housework, aren't they?
You will tell him, won't you?
He's going to win the race, isn't he?
You paid for the meal, didn't you?
She has forgotten the keys, hasn't she?
They had already left, hadn't they?
You can come to the party, can't you?

He isn't very happy, is he?
He doesn't have a car, does he?
We aren't leaving already, are we?
We won't be late, will we?
You aren't going to pay me, are you?
She didn't stay till the end, did she?
I haven't upset you, have I?
You had never been there before, had you?
He can't help you tonight, can he?

We make tag questions with an auxiliary verb and a pronoun.
David likes tennis, doesn't he?

When the sentence is affirmative, we use a negative tag question.
He is right, isn't he?

When the sentence is negative, we use an affirmative tag question.
Susan isn't ready, is she?

The tag question for *I am* is *aren't I?*
I'm late, aren't I?

We use tag questions:

➤ to ask for confirmation of an opinion.
This party is great, isn't it?

➤ when we are sure about what we are saying.
You're Mary's daughter, aren't you?
(You look like your mother.)

1 ▶ **Complete the sentences with is, isn't, are or aren't.**

Ex. *You aren't angry, ...are...... you?*

1 She is very tall, ... she?

2 I'm late, ... I?

3 We .... going to miss the movie, aren't we?

4 He .... lying, is he?

5 You .... paying attention, are you?

6 They are very annoying, ... they?

2 ▶ **Match.**

Ex. *You forgot,*   a   doesn't she?

1   They didn't come,   b   won't you?

2   She hasn't read the article,   c   did they?

3   You will tell me the truth,   d   *didn't you?*

4   I can call her,   e   can't I?

5   He won't help me,   f   has she?

6   She likes him a lot,   g   will he?

3 ▶ **Complete the sentences.**

Ex. ......*I'm not*...... *boring you, am I?*

1   .... listening to the policeman, was he?

2   .... going to buy a new car, aren't they?

3   .... to the same school as my mother, didn't you?

4   .... afford a new laptop, can we?

5   .... like playing baseball, does he?

6   .... played well today, have they?

7   .... starting to learn English, isn't he?

8   .... watch television very often, do they?

4 ▶ **Complete the sentences with a tag question from the box.**

| aren't we?   can we?   did they?   did we?   didn't they? |
| has he?   hasn't he?   is she?   isn't she? |

Ex. *She isn't enjoying the movie,* ....*is she?*............

1   We're having chicken for dinner tonight, ...

2   She's living with her parents at the moment, ...

3   They went on vacation last summer, ...

4   He has been to China and India, ...

5   We didn't try hard enough, ...

6   He hasn't been working at the bank very long, ...

7   They didn't learn any Spanish while they were on vacation, ...

8   We can't wait much longer, ...

> **Think**about**it**
>
> If the first part of the sentence is negative, the question tag will be affirmative. If the first part of the sentence is affirmative, the question tag will be negative.

5 ▶ **Write the tag questions for the sentences.**

Ex. *Los Angeles is far from New York,* ....*isn't it?*............

1   He failed the test, ...

2   They're going to town tomorrow, ...

3   New Delhi is the capital of India, ...

4   You're not very interested in this, ...

5   She can speak Chinese really well, ...

6   I told you that already, ...

7   Kangaroos live in Australia, ...

8   He hasn't finished the report, ...?

Information Questions

We use information questions when we want to know more than *yes* or *no*. We make them with the question words *who*, *what*, *when*, *where*, *which*, *whose*, *why* and *how*.

Who

We use *who* to ask about people.
Who is going to the movie with you? (Matthew.)
Who is that woman? (My sister.)

What

We use *what* to ask about things or actions.
What are you carrying in that basket? (A cat.)
What does he do on Saturdays? (He plays football.)

When

We use *when* to ask about time.
When did you move here? (Last year.)
When will he be ready? (Soon.)

Where

We use *where* to ask about place.
Where have you been? (At the mall.)
Where did you buy that dress? (In New York.)

Which

We use *which* to ask about one person or thing within a group of similar people or things.
Which girl is your sister? (The one with the long hair.)
Which T-shirt will you buy? (The red one.)

Whose

We use *whose* to ask who something belongs to.
Whose car is this? (David's)
Whose birthday is it? (Mine)

Why

We use *why* to ask about the reason for something.
Why didn't he come to the party? (Because he was working.)
Why are they here? (Because they want to speak to you.)

How

We use *how* to ask about the way someone does something or to ask about someone's health.
How does he drive a car? (Very carefully)
How is he? (He's much better now, thanks.)

We can use *how* with adjectives and adverbs.
How old are you? (Thirty.)
How many units did you read? (All of them.)
How fast can he run? (Very fast.)
How quickly can you get here? (In five minutes.)

6 ▶ **Choose the correct answer.**

Ex. Who / How did you like India?

1   Who / Whose house are you going to stay in?

2   Why / When don't you study harder?

3   What / Which are you going to study?

4   When / Which university are you going to go to?

5   Where / When is she leaving?

6   What / How do you usually do in the evenings?

7   When / Where were you this afternoon?

8   Why / Which can't you meet me tonight?

7 ▶ **Complete the sentences with the words in the box.**

how (x2)   what   when (x2)   which   who   whose   why

Ex. ....*What*........ did you do last night?

1 .... did you first meet Tim?

2 .... aren't you coming to my dinner party?

3 .... will you know when it's time to leave?

4 .... pair of shoes did you buy?

5 .... wallet is this? Steve's or Al's?

6 .... do you think the party will finish?

7 .... is going to come out with us tonight?

8 .... can you finish all this work?

8 ▶ **Choose the correct answer.**

Ex. .... did he do on his birthday?
   a When   **b** Where   ⓒ What

1 .... book are you going to read first?
   a Who   **b** Which   **c** Why

2 .... did you break your leg?
   a Whose   **b** How   **c** Which

3 .... cut your hair?
   a Who   **b** Where   **c** When

4 .... car will you take?
   a Who   **b** When   **c** Whose

5 .... aren't you coming to the beach with us?
   a When   **b** Why   **c** Where

6 .... have you put my umbrella?
   a Where   **b** Why   **c** When

7 .... was the name of your friend again?
   a Who   **b** How   **c** What

8 .... are we going to get there? The car's broken.
   a What   **b** How   **c** Why

Subject / Object Questions

Subject Questions

When we are asking about the subject of a sentence, the word order does not change.
Who made lunch? (Angela made lunch.)
Which bag is the biggest? (The red one is.)

Object Questions

When we ask about the object of a sentence, the word order changes to question form.
Who does he want to marry? (He wants to marry Jane.)
What did he find on the beach? (He found a bracelet.)

9 ▶ **Write SQ for subject question and OQ for object question.**

Ex. *Who stole the car?* ___SQ___

1 Whose car did they steal? _____

2 Where did you go? _____

3 Who gave Jenny the book? _____

4 Who bought you those red roses? _____

5 How many pizzas did you order? _____

6 Which CD do you want to listen to? _____

7 What have you bought today? _____

8 Who took him to the museum? _____

10 ▶ **Write questions.**

Ex. *Where* ...*did Gordon take you?*...................
   Gordon took me to the grocery store.

1 Where ....
   They bought their new furniture at the mall.

2 Why ....
   I had a party because it was my birthday.

3 Who ....
   My sister plays chess really well.

4 What ....
   They lost their camera and some money.

5 Whose ....
   It's Norman's car.

6 Who ....
   We're going on vacation next month.

So / Neither

Tense	So	Neither
Simple Present: *to be*	She's lazy. So am I.	He isn't happy. Neither is she.
Simple Present	I like rock music. So do I.	I don't live in this town. Neither do we.
Present Continuous	I'm studying French. So is he.	Emma isn't watching TV. Neither am I.
Present Perfect	Jessie has gone to bed. So have the children.	I haven't seen him. Neither has she.
The Future with *Will*	We will go on Saturday. So will we.	I won't help you. Neither will I.
Simple Past	Toby came to the party. So did Sam.	We didn't bring a present. Neither did we.
Past Perfect	She had left. So had he.	They hadn't forgotten. Neither had we.
Can (modals)	I can swim. So can I.	She can't speak English. Neither can he.

When we want to agree with an affirmative sentence, we use *so* + auxiliary verb + subject.
She lives in Boston.
So does Bob.

When the main sentence doesn't have an auxiliary verb, we use *do, does* or *did* accordingly.
I like rock music.
So do I. / So does Jim.

When we want to agree with a negative sentence, we use *neither* + auxiliary verb + subject.
I don't like spinach.
Neither do I.

11 ▶ Complete the sentences with **so** or **neither**.

Ex. *We aren't very happy.*
......*Neither*...... *are we.*

1 I can ride a horse.
.... can I.

2 We don't live in this neighborhood.
.... do we.

3 She hasn't finished her work.
.... has John.

4 Diane told the truth.
.... did Will.

5 I'm tired.
.... am I.

12 ▶ Complete the sentences.

Ex. *I love playing computer games.*
......*So do*...... *I.*

1 We can't come to the party.
.... we.

2 They missed the bus.
.... I.

3 She didn't remember anything.
.... Jeff.

4 You haven't finished your lunch.
.... Bob.

5 Mary wants a new bicycle.
.... Peggy.

13 ▶ Find the mistakes and write the sentences correctly.

Ex. *When is he going on Saturday?*
Where is he going on Saturday? ....

1 She has three children, isn't she?
....

2 Who jacket is this?
....

3 "They don't like it here." "Neither we do."
....

4 Which color is your new coat?
....

5 Whose T-shirt will you wear: the black one or the white one?
....

6 He's been ill recently, wasn't he?
....

Thinkaboutit

When we use **have** or **has** in the Simple Present in the main part of the sentence, we use **don't** or **doesn't** in the tag question.

14 ▸ **Put a check (✓) next to the correct sentence.**

Ex. *Whose owns that red car outside?* _____
Who owns that red car outside? _✓_

1 How times does he go fishing every week? _____
How many times does he go fishing every week? _____

4 Which dog has he taken to the vet? _____
Who dog has he taken to the vet? _____

2 You aren't feeling sick, are you? _____
You aren't feeling sick, aren't you? _____

5 Whose gave you this book about dinosaurs? _____
Who gave you this book about dinosaurs? _____

3 What have you left your books? _____
Where have you left your books? _____

6 I'm too late, amn't I? _____
I'm too late, aren't I? _____

15 ▸ **Match.**

Ex. *What* ———— a does the party start?
1 Who ———— b *are you going to wear to the party?*
2 How   c are you going on vacation with?
3 Whose   d old is she?
4 Where   e are you going on vacation without me?
5 When   f birthday is it?
6 Why   g did you put my keys?

Pairwork

Work with a partner.
Ask questions about
your partner's family.
Use tag questions.

Writing

Your friend has just moved to a new city in a different country. Write an e-mail asking about the new home
and the city he or she has moved to.

87

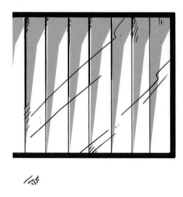

HE SHOULD LEARN HOW TO FILE.

Should for Advice

Affirmative

I/you should listen
he/she/it should listen
we/you/they should listen

Negative

I/you should not (shouldn't) listen
he/she/it should not (shouldn't) listen
we/you/they should not (shouldn't) listen

Question

Should I/you listen?
Should he/she/it listen?
Should we/you/they listen?

Short Answers

Yes, I/you should.   No, I/you shouldn't.
Yes, he/she/it should.   No, he/she/it shouldn't.
Yes, we/you/they should.   No, we/you/they shouldn't.

Should is a modal verb. It has only one form and does not add *-s* with *he*, *she* or *it*. We use the base form of a verb after it.
You should come and see us more often.
We shouldn't eat so much chocolate.

We use *should*:

➤ to give advice.
   She should study harder.
   He shouldn't speak to her like that.

➤ to ask for advice.
   Should I buy a new stereo?
   Should we go out or stay home tonight?

---

1 ▶ **Write sentences.**

Ex. *I don't understand what you're saying.*
     (listen / more carefully)
     You should listen more carefully.

1 He's very tired. (go to bed / early)
   ....

2 They're thirsty. (drink / more water)
   ....

3 I feel sick! (not eat / lots of chocolate)
   ....

4 She can't cook. (buy / a cookbook)
   ....

5 They don't have any money.
   (not buy / expensive gifts)
   ....

2 ▶ **Write questions.**

Ex. *I / buy / the book / the CD*
     Should I buy the book or the CD?

1 they / study / English / French
   ....

2 we / paint / the living room / the kitchen
   ....

3 I / go to college / get a job
   ....

4 they / watch / football / tennis
   ....

5 I / drink / coffee / tea
   ....

May / Might for Possibility

Affirmative
I/you may/might visit
he/she/it may/might visit
we/you/they may/might visit

Negative
I/you may not/might not visit
he/she/it may not/might not visit
we/you/they may not/might not visit

Notes

May and *might* are modal verbs. They have only one form and do not add *-s* with *he*, *she* or *it*. We use the base form of a verb after them.

We use *may* and *might* for possiblity.
It may be warm tomorrow.
The boss might be late today.

We often use short answers with *may* and *might* to answer *Yes/No* questions with *will*.
Will he call you later?   *Will you quit your job?*
He may. / He may not.   *I might. / I might not.*

We sometimes use *might* (but not *may*) in information questions.
What might happen to him?
He might lose his job.

---

3 ▶ **Write answers with may or might.**

Ex.   *Where's Pete? (in the kitchen)*
      He may be in the kitchen. / He might be in the kitchen.

1   Why is the baby crying? (hungry)

     ....

2   Where's the cat? (under the bed)

     ....

3   Who's at the door? (my friend Natasha)

     ....

4   Where are my keys? (on the chair)

     ....

5   How will they get to Mount Rushmore? (rent a car)

     ....

---

4 ▶ **Complete the sentences with might not or should.**

Ex.   *Mary is tired. She ......should...... go to bed now.*

1   The teacher is upset. We .... be quiet and not talk.

2   We're going out now. We .... be home until 11 o'clock.

3   Don't call Dan. He .... be awake yet.

4   You .... tell her about the accident.

5   That computer .... work because it's very old.

6   You .... go to the dentist every six months.

7   I .... wear my jacket. It's really hot today.

8   We .... always be polite to the customers.

5 ▸ **Choose the correct answer.**

Ex. *You .... stay home. Take a walk!*
a *should*   **b** *might*   ©*shouldn't*

1   I .... have enough money for both CDs,
    so I'll just buy one.
    a may   **b** might not   **c** shouldn't

2   We .... go out without our umbrellas. It's raining.
    a should   **b** shouldn't   **c** might

3   I .... have some money to lend you. Let me look
    in my wallet.
    a shouldn't   **b** may not   **c** might

4   We .... have lunch in the park today; the weather
    is perfect.
    a may   **b** shouldn't   **c** might not

5   He looks hurt. He .... have a broken leg.
    a should   **b** may   **c** shouldn't

6   There's the doorbell! It .... be Rita and her
    husband.
    a might   **b** should   **c** may not

6 ▸ **Check (✓) the correct sentence.**

Ex. *We may to go to the fast food restaurant.* _____
     We may go to the fast food restaurant. __✓__

1   People should be throw trash on the streets. _____
    People shouldn't throw trash on the streets. _____

2   He may not have eaten lunch yet. _____
    He should have eaten lunch yet. _____

3   You don't like spaghetti, so you should go to the Italian restaurant. _____
    You don't like spaghetti, so you shouldn't go to the Italian restaurant. _____

4   Do you think it shouldn't be expensive to fly to India? _____
    Do you think it might be expensive to fly to India? _____

5   He shouldn't eat so many sweets! He'll ruin his teeth. _____
    He might not eat so many sweets! He'll ruin his teeth. _____

6   He shouldn't like her cooking. _____
    He might not like her cooking. _____

7 ▸ **Complete the second sentence so that it has a similar meaning to the first. Use the word in parentheses in your answer.**

Ex. *It's possible that Neil wants a cup of coffee now. (might)*
     Neil .... might want .... a cup of coffee now.

1   It isn't a good idea to go to bed at 12 o'clock every night. (go)
    You .... at 12 o'clock every night.

2   It's possible that Karen isn't home now. (may)
    Karen .... now.

3   It's a good idea to exercise three times a week. (should)
    You .... three times a week.

4   Do you think it's possible that he is at work today? (be)
    Do you think he .... today?

5   The doctor told me to eat more fruits and vegetables. (should)
    The doctor said that I .... fruits and vegetables.

6   It is dangerous to use a cell phone when driving a car. (talk)
    You .... on a cell phone when you are driving.

Think about **it**

We always use the base
form of the verb after a
modal verb such as
should, **may** or **might**.

8 ▶ **Complete the sentences in your own words.**

Ex. *Where is your friend now?*
    He might ..*be at work.*..

1 George doesn't work very hard.

   He should ....

2 I heard a noise outside.

   It might ....

3 We want to drive to California, but our car is 12 years old.

   The car might ....

4 The teacher isn't here.

   He may ....

5 Lisa has had a fever for two days.

   She should ....

6 Kate isn't at work yet.

   She might ....

Pairwork

Work with a partner. Take turns asking for and giving advice. Think of three situations each. For example:

A: I want a new job, but I don't know how to get one. What should I do?

B: You should buy a newspaper and read the "Help Wanted" ads.

Writing

Your friend is going on a long trip around the world. Write a letter giving him/her advice. Say what your friend should bring and what places he/she should visit. Then suggest things he/she shouldn't do. Finally, talk about what might happen on the trip.

Dear ....,

It was great to get your letter. Your trip sounds very exciting! You asked me for some advice. Here it is!

I think you should ....

....

....

However, you shouldn't ....

....

....

You might ....

....

....

I hope you have a great time. Don't forget to send me a postcard!

....

15 First & Second Conditionals

First Conditional

We form the first conditional as follows:

If + Simple Present (*if* clause), Future with *will* (main clause)
If you go to bed late, you'll be tired in the morning.
If he doesn't go to college, he won't get a good job.

We use the first conditional to describe something
that will probably happen in the present or in the future.

Notes

When the *if* clause is before the main clause,
we use a comma.
If you help me move, I'll buy you dinner.

When the *if* clause is after the main clause,
we don't use a comma.
I'll buy you dinner if you help me move.

1 ▶ **Complete the sentences with the Simple Present.**

Ex. *If your team* ....*plays*............ *well, they will win the game. (play)*

1 We will go out now if you .... ready. (be)

2 He will wash the car if it .... (not rain)

3 If they .... to see a movie, we will stay at home. (not want)

4 If I .... my finals, I will graduate this summer. (pass)

5 We won't come to your house if you .... us to. (not want)

2 ▶ **Complete the sentences with *will* and the words in parentheses.**

Ex. *If the policeman catches the thief, he* ....*will send*............ *him to jail. (send)*

1 I .... you find an apartment if you decide to move. (help)

2 If you don't iron your clothes, they .... nice. (not look)

3 If she doesn't finish the report today, her boss .... angry. (be)

4 James .... on time if he doesn't go to bed now. (not get up)

5 They .... you if you don't speak clearly. (not understand)

3 ▶ **Write sentences in the first conditional.**

Ex. *you make lunch / I wash the dishes*
If you make lunch, I'll wash the dishes.

1 it snows / we go skiing

2 I hear a noise outside / I call the police

3 the restaurant is open / they eat dinner there

4 you send me an e-mail / I reply immediately

5 you read this book / you learn a lot about science

6 you not do your work / your boss not be pleased

4 ▶ **Write answers in the first conditional.**

Ex. *What will we do if the sun comes out? (we go swimming)*
If the sun comes out, we'll go swimming.

1 What will he do if he fails math? (take it again)

2 What will you do if there is an earthquake? (stand in the doorway)

3 What will they do if their friend is sick? (take him to the doctor)

4 What will we do if it rains tomorrow? (stay home)

5 What will you do if somebody steals your bike? (tell the police)

6 What will she do if she gets a new job? (buy a house)

Second Conditional

We form the second conditional as follows:

If + Simple Past (*if* clause), *would* + base form of verb (main clause)
If he got the job, he would move to Los Angeles.
If she were very rich, she would buy a big house.

We use the second conditional:

➤ to talk about something that is impossible in the present or in the future.
If you were a child, you would enjoy this cartoon.

➤ to talk about something that is possible in the present or in the future but is unlikely to happen.
If I won the lottery, I would buy an airplane.

➤ to give advice.
If I were you, I'd apologize to her.

Notes

In main clauses with *be*, we usually use *were* (and not *was*) when the subject is *I*, *he*, *she* or *it*.
If I were you, I wouldn't tell him.
If Sam were here, he would help you.

5 ▶ **Write sentences in the second conditional.**

Ex. *If I won a prize (I give it to my daughter)*
If I won a prize, I would give it to my daughter.
....

1 If there was a storm (she be frightened)
....

2 If she went to college (she study science)
....

3 If he played better (be on the school team)
....

4 If we looked after the environment (the world be a more beautiful place)
....

5 If everybody were kind to animals (I feel very happy)
....

6 If the movie were longer (I go to sleep)
....

6 ▶ **Write answers.**

Ex. *What would you do if you lost your dog? (look for it)*
If I lost my dog, I would look for it.
....

1 What would you do if your house fell down? (find a new one)
....

2 What would you do if your tooth hurt? (go to the dentist)
....

3 What would you do if you were late for work? (apologize to the manager)
....

4 What would you do if you had your own airplane? (fly around the world)
....

5 What would you do if your son broke his arm? (take him to the hospital)
....

6 What would you do if you were on vacation? (get up late every morning)
....

7 ▶ Complete the sentences in the second conditional.

Ex. Anthony ....*would be*........ very happy if his team ....*won*............ the championship. (be, win)

1 If I .... all the housework, my wife .... very surprised. (do, be)

2 My friend .... lots of new clothes if he .... more money. (buy, have)

3 If we .... too much food, then we .... sick. (eat, feel)

4 My friend .... us every day if he .... near us. (visit, live)

5 I .... to your house if I .... a car. (come, have)

6 If they .... it was a good idea, they .... their house and move to the country. (think, sell)

Thinkabout**it**

We never use **would** in the **if** clause. We use the Simple Past.

8 ▶ Join the two sentences. Use the second conditional.

Ex. *We have a pool. We go swimming every day.*
If we didn't have a pool, we wouldn't go swimming every day.

1 I eat fruit and vegetables every day. I'm very healthy.
....

2 I read a book every day. My eyes hurt.
....

3 My friends are the same age as me. They like the same music.
....

4 Her job is boring. She wants to quit.
....

5 Sally works hard. Her boss is pleased with her.
....

6 John speaks Japanese. He works for an American firm in Tokyo.
....

9 ▶ Write **1st** if the sentence is in the first conditional and **2nd** if it is in the second conditional.

Ex. *If Martin comes, will you tell him that I am in the shower?* __1st__

1 If I won the lottery, I would be amazed! _____

2 Will you wash the car if I clean the kitchen? _____

3 Would you buy a sports car if you had enough money? _____

4 I wouldn't be surprised if he failed the driving test. _____

5 If I were you, I wouldn't wear jeans to the job interview. _____

6 Will they go skiing if it snows? _____

7 If it isn't cold, we'll take the dog for a long walk this evening. _____

8 He would be upset if you told him the truth. _____

10 ▶ **Find the extra word in each sentence and write it on the dotted line.**

Ex.   *What would you have do if you saw a big spider?* ....*have*........

1   If I would have enough money, I will buy everyone a present. ....

2   Would you to look after my dog if I went away for a few days? ....

3   He won't get a pay raise if he doesn't not work hard. ....

4   Will you be come to my party if I invite you? ....

5   If I moved to Brazil, would you do miss me? ....

6   Would you wear that coat if I will bought it for you? ....

7   If I were being you, I would get a hair cut. ....

8   Will you cook dinner this evening if I would bring the food? ....

11 ▶ **Choose the correct answer.**

Ex.   *I wouldn't drink that milk if I* .... *you.*
      a *wasn't*   **ⓑ** *were*   **c** *am*

1   If I'm tired, ... go to bed at 10 o'clock.
    a I'm   **b** I'd   **c** I'll

2   .... you lend me some money if I promised to pay you back?
    a Would   **b** Will   **c** Were

3   Will you remind me to buy bread if I ....?
    a forgot   **b** forget   **c** forgotten

4   If I get a taxi home, will you .... for it?
    a pay   **b** paid   **c** to pay

5   .... buy a new sports car if he had more money.
    a He will   **b** He had   **c** He would

6   If I were you, I .... be nice to my friends.
    a would   **b** will   **c** won't

12 ▶ **Put a check (✓) next to the sentence with the same meaning as the first.**

Ex.   *I would help you with your work if I understood it better.*
      a *I won't help you because I don't understand your work well.* __✓__
      b *I will help you because I understand your work better than you.* _____

1   He would buy a new house if he had the money.
    a He has enough money for a new house. _____
    b He doesn't have enough money for a new house. _____

2   If she weren't a nice person, she wouldn't have many friends.
    a She has a lot of friends because she's nice. _____
    b She doesn't have a lot of friends because she isn't nice. _____

3   If I feel worse, I will go to the doctor.
    a I may go to the doctor. _____
    b I should go to the doctor. _____

4   My cousins would go skiing more often if they had more time.
    a My cousins have a lot of time to ski. _____
    b My cousins don't have a lot of time to ski. _____

13 ▶ **Find the mistakes and write the sentences correctly.**

Ex.   *If I don't sleep enough tonight, I would feel tired in the morning.*
      If I don't sleep enough tonight, I will feel tired in the morning.

1   I will lend you money if you will need some.

   ....

2   Would you take me to the party if I come to your house?

   ....

3   I will watch television all evening if there be some good shows on.

   ....

4   I would feel sick if I eaten all that chocolate.

   ....

5   If it will rain tomorrow, we didn't go swimming.

   ....

6   Will you feel frightened if you saw an alien?

   ....

Pairwork

Work with a partner. Take turns. Ask and answer three questions beginning with *What will you do if ... ?* and three questions with *What would you do if ... ?* Use your imagination and have some fun!

For example:
What will you do if you lose your keys?
If I lose my keys, I'll break down the door!

What would you do if you saw a mouse?
If I saw a mouse, I'd faint!

Writing

Think of things you would like to do if you could. For example:

➤ travel around the world
➤ learn a new language
➤ buy a big house

Now think about what you would need to do these things. Write a paragraph about what you would do.

What I would do if I could!

....

....

....

....

....

....

....

....

....

....

....

Prepositions of Place

We use prepositions of place to talk about where something or someone is.

at	near
behind	next to
between	on
in	opposite
in front of	under

I left my cell phone at work.
Turn around. There's a mouse behind you!
Put the letter in the envelope.
The cat is in front of the fireplace.
Do you live in the house next to Julie's?
Mike works near the park on Main Street.
I found my keys! They were under my bed.
The butcher is between the bank and the library, just opposite the park.

1 ▷ Complete the sentences with in or on.

Ex.   *The books are* ...*on*.... *the table.*

1   My money is .... my purse.

2   The vase is .... the television.

3   Do you have a lot of furniture .... your house?

4   There is some milk .... the refrigerator.

5   The cat is sleeping .... the chair.

6   Have you put your clothes .... the closet?

7   Look at all those clouds .... the sky!

8   Let's hang the picture .... the wall.

2 ▷ Choose the correct answer.

Ex.   *I was born* in / *opposite California.*

1   Your shoes are *under / between* your desk.

2   Do you sit *next to / on* Barbara in English class?

3   There is a supermarket *between / opposite* my house.

4   Is your brother *at / on* work today?

5   He had an accident because the car *under / in front of* him stopped suddenly.

6   Is there a bank *between / near* your office?

7   I found my keys. They were *between / opposite* the sofa cushions.

8   I can't see Jane. She might be in the yard *under / behind* the house.

Prepositions of Time

We use prepositions of time to talk about when something happens.

We use *in* for:

➤ months   *We're getting married in June.*
➤ years   *He died in 1988.*
➤ centuries   *Did people have telephones in the 1800s?*
➤ seasons   *He takes a vacation in the summer.*
➤ periods of time   *I drink coffee in the morning and tea in the afternoon.*

We use *at* for:

➤ exact times   *The film starts at 9 o'clock.*
➤ points of time in a day   *She has her lunch at noon.*
➤ holidays and celebrations   *We usually dance at birthday parties.*

We use *on* for:

➤ days of the week   *He does his shopping on Saturdays.*
➤ dates   *It's my birthday on April 9th.*
➤ celebrations and holidays with   *We don't work on New Year's Day.*
   the word *day* in them

Notes

We say *in the morning, in the afternoon* and *in the evening,* but *at night.*

---

3 ▶ **Complete the sentences with in, at or on.**

Ex. *He will be thirteen ...on.... September 6th.*

1   I like going for walks .... night.
2   What are you doing .... Sunday?
3   I'll meet you outside the museum .... the morning.
4   It's hot .... the summer.

5   What did you do .... her wedding?
6   Where do you go .... New Year's Eve?
7   Is your birthday .... March or April?
8   The party will finish .... 11 o'clock.

Prepositions of Movement

We use prepositions of movement to express motion.

across	to
along	through
down	toward
from	up

The children ran across the street.
We walked along the river.
I looked down the street and saw her coming from the bank.
Are you going to the post office later?
He threw the ball through the open window.
Who's that man coming toward us?
The squirrel ran up the tree.

4 ▶ **Choose the correct answer.**

Ex. *Could you go up /(to) the drugstore for me, please?*

1   Why is he running *from / along* the train tracks?
2   I don't like going *toward / up* ladders.
3   You must never walk *across / through* the street without looking.
4   The train is going *from / through* the tunnel.
5   What time are you coming home *to / from* school today?
6   Let's go *to / toward* the mall on Saturday.

5 ▶ **Complete the sentences with the correct preposition.**

Ex. *We always eat a lot ......on...... Sunday!*

1   What do you do .... the evening?
2   Do you go .... the movies every week?
3   Who is that .... the door?
4   Will you be here .... 8 o'clock in the morning?
5   I'm not climbing .... all those stairs!
6   I can't swim .... the river. It's more than a mile to the other side!

Reflexive Pronouns

myself	ourselves
yourself	yourselves
himself	themselves
herself	
itself	

We use reflexive pronouns:

➤ when the object and the subject of a sentence are the same.
She watched herself on TV.
He's talking to himself!

➤ with certain verbs (*behave, cut, enjoy, hurt*, etc).
Children, behave yourselves!
He cut himself while he was shaving.
Are they enjoying themselves in Hawaii?
Did you hurt yourself?

➤ with the verb *help* when it means "take something" (e.g., food or drink).
Please help yourselves to more coffee.
Can I help myself to a piece of cake?

➤ when we say someone did something without another person's help.
I made this dress myself.
Did he do his work himself?

If we want to emphasize that we did something without help or to show that we did something alone, we can use *by* or *all by* before the reflexive pronoun.
She went on vacation by herself. She prefers traveling alone.
I learned to speak Spanish all by myself. I didn't take lessons.

---

6 ▷ **Complete the sentences with the words from the box.**

I	my son	the dog	they
you	your daughter	we	

Ex. ....*My son*............ went to Australia by himself.

1 Has .... ever repaired the car by herself?

2 .... can't do all the housework by myself.

3 Are .... going to enjoy themselves in the park?

4 .... organized the concert by ourselves.

5 Did .... make all those cakes yourself?

6 Is .... sitting outside in the rain by itself?

---

7 ▷ **Complete the sentence with the correct reflexive pronoun.**

Ex. *Our cat doesn't like playing by ....itself........... .*

1 Did they enjoy .... at the concert?

2 Is he going to drive to Milan by ....?

3 Janet blamed .... for losing the dog.

4 Be careful! You might cut ....!

5 I hate .... for not sending you a birthday card.

6 We taught .... to play chess.

8 ▷ **Choose the correct answer.**

Ex. *Shall I put the new rug .... the sofa?*
  a in   **b** in front of   **c** at

1 I don't think we can get that big table .... the door.
  a along   **b** down   **c** through

2 Will you be awake at 6 o'clock .... the morning?
  a in   **b** on   **c** at

3 Can your children make lunch by ....?
  a yourself   **b** themselves   **c** yourselves

4 I'll be .... vacation in August.
  a in   **b** to   **c** on

5 I'm late because the bus left .... 3 o'clock today.
  a at   **b** to   **c** from

6 The baby boy walked by .... for the first time yesterday!
  a herself   **b** himself   **c** itself

> **9** Find the mistakes and write the sentences correctly.

Ex. *Why don't you clean up your room myself?*

   Why don't you clean up your room yourself? ....

1 Will you give Vicky her present in her birthday?

   ....

2 Why don't we go skiing from December this year?

   ....

3 Is he doing the report herself?

   ....

4 Who is that standing next on your son?

   ....

5 I can't see across these windows. They're very dirty!

   ....

6 Were you born on 1990?

   ....

Pairwork

Work with a partner. Take turns. Talk about yourself.
What are the things you can do by yourself?
What are the things you prefer to do by yourself?

Writing

Write a description of a place you know well on a busy Saturday morning. Use as many different prepositions as you can.

....

....

....

....

....

....

....

....

....

....

....

....

Review 4 (Units 13-16)

1 ▶ Write tag questions for the sentences.

Ex. *The cat is playful,* .....*isn't it?*.............

1 You're an English teacher, ...

2 I'm good at playing tennis, ...

3 He doesn't work very hard, ...

4 They broke the computer, ...

5 We're having fun, ...

6 Let's buy a pizza, ...

7 She can't ski, ...

8 You haven't washed the car, ...

9 You drink a lot of milk, ...

10 The children aren't cold, ...

3 ▶ Match.

Ex. *Where did Phil see Paul?*   a   Her boyfriend did.

1 Who will make breakfast?   b   *At the museum.*

2 Who gave Sarah roses?   c   Jason does.

3 Who's going to go with him?   d   For the wedding.

4 What has he bought a suit for?   e   A diamond ring.

5 Who has a beard?   f   Henry is.

6 What did he give her?   g   Zoe will.

2 ▶ Write questions.

Ex. *Where* .....*did you see Peter?*.....................................
I saw Peter at the art gallery.

1 Which ....
I bought the striped dress.

2 How ....
He goes to work by train.

3 Where ....
We spent the evening at Debbie's house.

4 What ....
We had chicken and potatoes for lunch.

5 Why ....
I left because I was tired.

6 When ....
I learned to drive two years ago.

7 How ....
I'm fine, thanks.

8 Whose ....
It's Peter's car.

4 ▶ Complete the sentences with so or neither and an auxiliary verb.

Ex. *I love eating ice cream.*
.........*So do*......... I.

1 We can't go shopping this afternoon.
.... we.

2 She doesn't want to come.
.... he.

3 They forgot their keys.
.... I.

4 She didn't eat any of her food.
.... Jeff.

5 You haven't finished your work.
.... Bob.

6 Mary wants to buy a present.
.... Peggy.

5 ▶ **Rewrite the sentences with should or shouldn't.**

Ex. *We are rude to the doctor.*
       We shouldn't be rude to the doctor.
....

1   He goes to bed late.

    ....

2   You don't eat enough vegetables.

    ....

3   People don't care about the environment.

    ....

4   You leave your dirty dishes on the table.

    ....

5   She doesn't drink lots of water every day.

    ....

6   You go out every night.

    ....

6 ▶ **Complete the sentences with may, might not, should or shouldn't.**

Ex. *It's snowing so he ....might not.......... visit us today.*

1   You .... exercise more and eat healthy food.
2   People .... be cruel to animals.
3   It .... be a good idea for Joe to live alone. He's very old.
4   You really .... eat six meals a day.
5   I didn't study much and I'm worried I .... pass the test.
6   Don't wait for me. I .... come.
7   You .... eat that banana. It's still green.
8   She .... want to see the movie because it's really good.
9   We'll go out if we can, but it .... rain.
10 I don't think you .... spend so much money.

7 ▶ **Choose the correct answer.**

Ex. *The phone's ringing. It .... be my friend Lee.*
    (a) *might*   **b** *shouldn't*   **c** *can*

1   He .... arrive late as there is a lot of traffic.
    a might not   **b** shouldn't   **c** may

2   The sun .... come out today.
    a might   **b** shouldn't   **c** may to

3   Do you think it .... snow?
    a shouldn't   **b** might   **c** might not

4   Everybody .... learn something new from time to time.
    a shouldn't   **b** might   **c** should

5   You .... speak to your parents like that!
    a shouldn't   **b** should   **c** might not

6   This computer .... work.
    a might not   **b** should not   **c** should be

7   People .... drive fast near schools.
    a might not   **b** shouldn't   **c** should

8   We .... work harder in English.
    a should   **b** might not   **c** shouldn't

8 ▶ **Complete the sentences with the first conditional.**

Ex. *If you say you're sorry, I ....will forgive....... you. (forgive)*

1   If you give me some money, I .... you a nice present. (buy)

2   They'll get into trouble if they .... work early. (leave)

3   If it rains this evening, we .... to the park. (not go)

4   The manager won't be happy if you .... the project on time. (not finish)

5   If I .... the car, will you make dinner? (wash)

6   If people continue polluting the environment, what ....? (happen)

7   Will you be angry if I .... lunch with you today? (not have)

8   What will you study if you .... to college? (go)

9 ▶ **Complete the sentences with the second conditional.**

Ex. *If you ....left.......... your keys on the bus, what would you do? (leave)*

1   If the temperature .... to five degrees, would you be happy? (fall)

2   What would you do if I .... you a lot of money? (give)

3   Would you feel sick if you .... a large pizza by yourself? (eat)

4   If they asked me, I .... them. (help)

5   Would your cell phone still work if you .... it on the floor? (drop)

6   How would you get to work if there .... any buses? (not be)

7   The world would be a better place if there .... so much pollution. (not be)

8   I would buy a new house if I .... more money. (have)

10 ▶ **Choose the correct answer.**

Ex. *If I .... the money, I would go on a cruise.*
    a would had   **b** would have   **c** had

1   What .... you do if you met a movie star?
    a if   **b** would   **c** did

2   If he buys you a diamond ring, ... you wear it?
    a would   **b** will   **c** do

3   I will cry .... I watch a sad movie.
    a would   **b** will   **c** if

4   If people don't stop hunting elephants, there .... be any left soon.
    a will   **b** wouldn't   **c** won't

5   If he .... drive, he would buy a a sports car.
    a could   **b** can   **c** would

6   I would .... to China if I had the chance.
    a went   **b** go   **c** had gone

7   If you stop crying, I .... take you to the park.
    a would   **b** won't   **c** will

8   What will you .... your boss if she asks you where you've been?
    a tell   **b** told   **c** will tell

11 ▸ **Choose the correct answer.**

Ex.   *The bowl of fruit is* in /(on)*the table.*

1   I'd like you to sit *at / between* Susan and me.
2   Sally is *at / to* home today.
3   We live *near / under* the swimming pool.
4   The dog must be frightened because he is hiding *under / opposite* the table.
5   They live in an apartment that is *at / opposite* the park.
6   Let's meet *at / on* the post office.
7   Don't walk right *near / in front of* me or I'll step on your foot!
8   The salt is *next to / in* the pepper on the table.
9   My best friend lives *to / in* Seattle.
10 No one will see you if you hide *between / behind* that tree!

12 ▸ **Complete the sentences with in, at or on.**

Ex.   *We moved here* .....*in*..... *1997.*

1   Is your birthday .... July or August?
2   She'll be home soon. She left the party .... midnight.
3   What are you doing .... New Year's Day?
4   What are you doing .... work today?
5   The game starts .... 7 o'clock tonight.
6   Does it snow here .... the winter?
7   My friend is getting married .... May 27th.
8   I'll see you .... Wednesday.
9   Was she born .... the twentieth century?
10 I think I'll go snowboarding .... the morning.

13 ▸ **Choose the correct answer.**

Ex.   *I am taking the train*(to)/ *towards Boston.*

1   All the children are going *down / to* the school.
2   Never walk *through / across* the road without looking both ways first.
3   It's not easy for her to walk *from / up* hills since she injured her knee.
4   Judy is coming *down / toward* the street with the baby in her arms.
5   We walked for miles *across / along* the path by the river.
6   He got lost coming home *from / toward* the farm.
7   I nearly walked *to / through* the glass door without opening it!
8   All the cars were driving *across / toward* the beach on Friday afternoon.

14 ▸ **Complete the sentences with the correct reflexive pronoun.**

Ex.   *The cat likes playing by* ....*itself*............. .

1   Did she enjoy .... at the party?
2   Is he going to Japan by ....?
3   We blamed .... for causing the accident.
4   Don't cut .... while you're cutting up those onions.
5   I hate .... for lying to him all this time.
6   They helped .... to some more cake.

17 Gerunds & Infinitives

Gerunds

We can use verbs with the *-ing* ending as nouns. We call them gerunds.

We can use gerunds:

➤ as the subject of a sentence.
Swimming is my favorite sport.
Sleeping is my favorite hobby!
Playing chess is a lot of fun.

➤ as the object of a sentence.
I like swimming.
I love sleeping!
I enjoy playing games.

➤ after prepositions.
Don't leave without saying goodbye.
She's not very good at playing tennis.
I'm interested in learning a new language.
Thank you for helping me.

We can also use the gerund with certain verbs and phrases.

can't help
can't stand
dislike
(don't) mind
enjoy
hate
like
love
miss

She can't help worrying about you.
They can't stand listening to loud music.
She dislikes waiting for the bus in the rain.
I don't mind looking after the children tonight.
They enjoy going to museums.

---

1 ▸ Complete the sentences using gerunds.

Ex. *He loves .....listening..... to loud music on his stereo. (listen)*

1   Do you mind .... the baby while I go out? (look after)

2   The chocolates are delicious. I can't help .... them! (eat)

3   Do you enjoy .... on the beach? (lie)

4   The twins are afraid of .... home in the dark. (walk)

5   They're not very good at .... business reports. (write)

6   He enjoys .... in the park every morning. (run)

7   She misses .... by the sea. (live)

8   You can't stand .... your homework, can you? (do)

2 ▶ **Complete the sentences with the words from the box. Use gerunds.**

| buy | do | go | learn | play | study | swim | walk | work |

Ex. *Do you like ......learning...... about English grammar?*

1 I can't help .... nice clothes.

2 I'm tired of .... I always lose.

3 I love .... in the forest on a sunny day.

4 We don't like .... the dishes.

5 He's very good at .... the backstroke.

6 I'm interested in .... engineering.

7 They enjoy .... to art museums.

8 She hates .... in an office.

3 ▶ **Put a check (✓) next to the correct sentence.**

Ex. *I can't help to cry when I watch a sad movie.* _____
I can't help crying when I watch a sad movie. __✓__

1 John hates going to the movies without me. _____
John hating to go to the movies without me. _____

2 They can't help to laughing at a funny joke. _____
They can't help laughing at a funny joke. _____

3 We enjoy sleeping late on Sundays. _____
We enjoy sleep late on Sundays. _____

4 I shouldn't leave without tell my boss. _____
I shouldn't leave without telling my boss. _____

5 Steve likes being a twin. _____
Steve likes be a twin. _____

6 Alfred can't give up the smoking. _____
Alfred can't give up smoking. _____

4 ▶ **Write sentences.**

Ex. *smoke / be / bad for your health*
Smoking is bad for your health............................

1 collect / stamps / be / my hobby
....

2 do / math / be / very difficult
....

3 go out / with friends / be / fun
....

4 water / the plants / keep / them alive
....

5 send / e-mails / be / easy
....

6 study / hard / be / tiring
....

Infinitives

We form the infinitive with *to* + the base form of the verb.
We use infinitives after certain verbs.

afford	offer
allow	persuade
ask	promise
decide	refuse
hope	want

He asked her to go to the movies with him.
They offered to lend us their car.
I persuaded her to come with me.
She refused to let me pay for the meal.

We also use infinitives after certain adjectives.

amazed	sad
glad	sorry
happy	surprised

She was sad to leave home.
I was surprised to see him at the party.

Notes

We can follow some verbs (e.g., *like, hate, love*) with either a gerund or infinitive; the meaning is the same.

I like walking in the rain.
I like to walk in the rain.

I hate studying history.
I hate to study history.

I love traveling by plane.
I love to travel by plane.

5 ▶ **Complete the sentences with the words from the box. Use infinitives.**

> buy   do   go   have
> help   study   watch

Ex.   *He was very kind and offered ......to help...... me with*
       my project.

1   The children are not allowed .... television
     after midnight.
2   They decided .... a party on Saturday night.
3   He persuaded me .... a new pair of jeans.
4   Peter refused .... any more work on the
     weekend.
5   She invited me .... on vacation with her.
6   I want .... in Toronto.

6 ▶ **Put a check (✓) next to the correct sentences.**

Ex.   *I don't mind to learn English. _____*
       They have decided to buy a new car. __✓__

1   Can you afford going to buy a new car? _____
2   He offered to take me to see the movie. _____
3   I persuaded Frank coming to the fair with us. _____
4   When she goes on vacation, she misses watching
     her favorite TV shows. _____
5   I'm so glad to see you again. _____
6   They want to learn Chinese. _____
7   I hope meeting you again soon. _____
8   You are not allowed going fishing in this river. _____
9   I can't stand watching scary movies. _____
10   He refused lending me any money. _____

7 ▶ **Complete the sentences with a gerund or infinitive. (More than one answer may be possible.)**

Ex.   *I don't mind ......working...... hard. (work)*

1   We promise .... home by 12 o'clock. (be)
2   He enjoys .... to basketball games. (go)
3   They were surprised .... him. (see)
4   I can't persuade him .... going to the gym. (start)
5   Denise asked me .... some bread from the bakery. (buy)
6   Do you like .... English books? (read)
7   They miss .... the food their grandmother used to make. (eat)
8   We want .... Sam something useful for his birthday. (get)

8 ▶ **Complete the sentences with the words from the box.**

> can't stand   decided   hope   learning   telling   to leave

Ex.   *He enjoys ......learning...... about space travel.*

1   They .... going to the zoo!
2   Have you .... to come with us to the museum?
3   Sarah was sad .... her friends.
4   I .... to travel a lot when I've saved up some money.
5   She doesn't believe in .... lies!

9 ▶ **Complete the sentences.**

Ex.   *I ......miss seeing...... our old neighbors. (miss / see)*

1   She .... , so she won't pass any of her tests. (refuse / study)
2   Do you .... at home sometimes? (enjoy / stay)
3   I .... with you to the doctor. (not mind / come)
4   He has .... with me to the dentist. (offer / come)
5   Some people .... shy! (can't help / be)
6   Do you .... harder next year? (promise / work)
7   He .... at 6:00 a.m., but sometimes he has to. (dislike / wake up)
8   Jennifer .... for his rudeness. (persuade him / apologize)

10 ▶ **Choose the correct answer.**

Ex.   *Do you enjoy .... the only male in your family?*
    a *to be*   **ⓑ** *being*   **c** *you are*

1   He hates .... letters.
    a writing   **b** written   **c** to be writing

2   I persuaded Jill .... me a lift to the mall.
    a giving   **b** to gave   **c** to give

3   I hope .... a new computer course next month.
    a to start   **b** start   **c** starting

4   Do you mind .... me with all this work?
    a to help   **b** doing   **c** helping

5   They can't help .... sorry for the team that lost.
    a feeling   **b** to feel   **c** to be

6   I dislike .... documentaries.
    a to watch   **b** to see   **c** watching

7   I'm sorry .... that you are leaving.
    a to hear   **b** hear   **c** hearing

8   Are you interested in .... to the game with me on Saturday?
    a coming   **b** to come   **c** will come

11 ▶ **Find the mistakes and write the sentences correctly.**

Ex.   *Swim is a great sport for keeping fit.*
    Swimming is a great sport for keeping fit.

1   He'll never stop smoke.
    ....

2   Have you decided to be quitting your job?
    ....

3   He doesn't mind plays games with his son.
    ....

4   Did she offer helping you with the cooking?
    ....

5   Am I allowed have another piece of cake?
    ....

6   I want writing a report about the environment.
    ....

12 ▶ **Complete the second sentence so that it has a similar meaning to the first sentence. Use the word in parentheses in your answer.**

Ex.   *I said I would tell the truth. (promised)*
    I .... promised to tell .... the truth.

1   "I'll help you wash the car," said Lucy. (offered)
    Lucy .... wash the car.

2   I hate to watch TV shows about hospitals. (stand)
    I .... TV shows about hospitals.

3   "No, I'm not going to the dentist," said Henry. (refused)
    Henry .... to the dentist.

4   I don't want to eat any cake because I don't like it. (enjoy)
    I .... cake.

5   "Can I borrow your car?" asked Donald. (asked)
    Donald .... my car.

13 ▶ **Complete the sentences in your own words.**

Ex.   *I can't afford ...to buy a new computer this year.................*

1   I am happy ....

2   I can't help ....

3   I love ....

4   I really hope ....

5   I don't mind ....

6   I really want ....

	love	like	dislike	can't stand
eat pizza				
watch scary movies				
listen to music				
swim in the ocean				
go shopping				
do housework				
wash the car				
go to a museum				

Pairwork

Check (✓) what is true for you in this chart. Work with a partner and tell him/her what you love, like, etc.

Writing

Your new penpal has written to you and asked about your likes and dislikes. Write an e-mail in response. Use gerunds and infinitives to describe your likes and dislikes.

	e-mail	

Send Now Send Later Save as Draft Add Attachments Signature ▼ Options ▼ Rewrap

From:
To:
Cc:
Bcc:
Subject:
Attachments: *none*

Default Font ▾ | Text Size ▾ | B I U T | ≡ ≡ ≡ | ≣ ≣ ≣ ≣ | A ▾ ◇ ▾ | —

Dear ....,

Thank you for your e-mail. It was nice to read all about you. Now I'm going to tell you a bit about me!

I enjoy doing lots of different things. I love ....

....

....

....

But I really don't like ....

....

....

....

When I have free time on the weekend, I enjoy ....

....

Please write again soon.

Best wishes,

....

Passive Voice: Introduction and Simple Present Passive (Affirmative)

Introduction

➤ In active voice sentences, the subject (or "agent") performs an action on an object (or "receiver" of the action).
Mike makes furniture.
Tom and Sue write poems.

➤ To place greater emphasis on the receiver and what happens to it, we use the passive voice. In passive voice sentences, the receiver is the subject. The agent (if there is one) comes at the end of the sentence after the word *by*.
Furniture is made by Mike.
Poems are written by Tom and Sue.

➤ We form passive voice verbs with the auxiliary verb *be* (in any tense) and the past participle of the main verb.

Simple Present Passive

Affirmative

I am employed	we are employed
you are employed	you are employed
he/she/it is employed	they are employed

We use the passive voice:

➤ when we want to emphasize the action rather than the agent.
He is driven to school by his mother.

➤ when we don't know the agent.
Many cars are stolen every year.

➤ when the agent is obvious.
English is spoken in many countries.
(by people)

1 ▶ **Complete the sentences with is or are.**

Ex. *Our car .....is..... serviced at an excellent garage.*

1   Milk .... kept in the refrigerator.

2   Penguins .... found in Antarctica.

3   Children .... taught to read in elementary school.

4   A librarian .... employed by a library.

5   Computers .... used everywhere nowadays.

6   *The New York Times* .... read around the world.

7   Cows and chickens .... raised on farms.

8   Rice .... eaten throughout Asia.

2 ► **Complete the sentences using Simple Present Passive.**

Ex. *Thieves* ....*are caught*.......... *by policemen. (catch)*

1   Clothes .... by tailors. (make)

2   Bread .... by bakers. (bake)

3   Paintings are .... by artists. (paint)

4   Cars .... by mechanics. (repair)

5   Houses .... by construction workers. (build)

6   The *Mona Lisa* .... by thousands of people every year. (see)

7   My hair .... by a hairdresser. (cut)

8   My eyes .... by an eye doctor. (test)

Simple Present Passive (Negatives, Questions and Short Answers)

Negative
I am not (I'm not) employed
you are not (aren't) employed
he/she/it is not (isn't) employed
we/you/they are not (aren't) employed

Question
Am I employed?
Are you employed?
Is he/she/it employed?
Are we/you/they employed?

Notes
To form short answers in the Simple Present Passive, we use a subject and the Simple Present form of *be*.
Is the report done?   *Are these seats taken?*
Yes, it is.   *No, they're not.*

---

3 ► **Make the sentences negative and write answers.**

Ex. *Yogurt is made from cheese. (milk)*
Yogurt isn't made from cheese.
Yogurt is made from milk.

1   T-shirts are made of wool. (cotton)
....
....

2   Honey is made by flies. (bees)
....
....

3   Tea is grown in Alaska. (India)
....
....

4   Meat is kept in the cupboard. (freezer)
....
....

5   Bank robbers are put in hotels. (prisons)
....
....

6   Race cars are driven by children. (adults)
....
....

4 ► **Write questions.**

Ex. *fruit / sell / the butcher / ?*
Is fruit sold by the butcher?

1   magazines / write / students / ?
....

2   candy / buy / children / ?
....

3   cars / make / robots / ?
....

4   Portuguese / speak / Brazilians / ?
....

5   tests / take / students / ?
....

6   snacks / eat / everyone / ?
....

Simple Past Passive

Affirmative	Negative	Question
I was robbed	I was not (wasn't) robbed	Was I robbed?
you were robbed	you were not (weren't) robbed	Were you robbed?
he/she/it was robbed	he/she/it was not (wasn't) robbed	Was he/she/it robbed?
we/you/they were robbed	we/you/they/were not (weren't) robbed	Were we/you/they robbed?

Short Answers

Yes, I was.	No, I wasn't
Yes, you were.	No you weren't.
Yes, he/she/it was.	No, he/she/it/ wasn't.
Yes, we/you/they were.	No, we/you/they weren't.

We form the SImple Past Passive with *was* or *were* and the past participle.

I was driven to work by a friend.   *We were given a present by Mike.*
(A friend drove me to work.)   (Mike gave us a present.)

---

5 ▶ **Complete the sentences with was or were.**

Ex.   *My daughter .....was..... hit by a tennis ball.*

1   The window .... broken by those boys.

2   The children .... helped by the teacher.

3   My dog .... fed by our neighbor last week.

4   Who .... the first plane made by?

5   The photographs .... taken by Janet.

6   Our house .... built a long time ago.

7   These chairs .... made by my grandfather.

8   The race .... won by Nick.

---

6 ▶ **Complete the sentences using Simple Past Passive.**

Ex.   *The fish ....was eaten......... by the cat. (eat)*

1   My computer crashed and it .... by a technician. (fix)

2   A lot of windows .... in last night's storm. (break)

3   Years ago computers .... only by big companies. (buy)

4   The present .... to me by Henry. (give)

5   At the party all the food .... by the guests. (eat)

6   The plays *Hamlet* and *Macbeth* .... by William Shakespeare. (write)

7   A shark .... by some fishermen yesterday. (catch)

8   The accident .... by a bad driver. (cause)

Think about it

Remember to use the past participle with the passive voice. For a list of irregular past participles, see the Irregular Verbs on page 102.

---

7 ▶ **Change the sentences from active to passive.**

Ex.   *Somebody damaged my car last week.*

   My car was damaged last week.
   ....

1   Mark painted our house last month.

   ....

2   The company bought new computers last month.

   ....

3   Someone stole my bag at the mall.

   ....

4   The police arrested the thief.

   ....

5   Denise made these curtains.

   ....

6   An Italian chef prepared this meal.

   ....

8 ▸ **Change the sentences from passive to active.**

Ex. *This table was made by my father.*

   My father made this table. ....

1   This watch was given to me by my best friend.

   ....

2   Her arm was X-rayed by the doctor.

   ....

3   Those flowers were given to the nurse by Billy.

   ....

4   Newspapers aren't sold in that shop.

   ....

5   Millions of hamburgers are sold by fast-food restaurants every year.

   ....

6   The Olympic Games were invented by the ancient Greeks.

   ....

9 ▸ **Choose the correct answer.**

Ex. *Pasta .... eaten in Italy.*

   a *be*   **(b)** *is*   **c** *does*

1   This car .... made in Korea.
   a are   **b** was   **c** has

2   Were your jeans .... at the mall?
   a buy   **b** buyed   **c** bought

3   .... your hair cut by a hairdresser?
   a Were   **b** Was   **c** Did

4   The prize was won .... John.
   a from   **b** of   **c** by

5   The flowers .... delivered by the florist.
   a were   **b** was   **c** been

6   The children were .... on vacation by their parents.
   a took   **b** take   **c** taken

10 ▸ **Complete the sentences with the past participle of the verbs from the box.**

| build | compose | destroy | discover | drown | hold | invent | make | write |

Ex. *My shoes are .... made .... of leather.*

1   Gold was .... by the miners.
2   Were the Olympics were .... in Greece in 2004?
3   The Empire State Building was .... in 1931.
4   Over fifteen hundred people were .... when the *Titanic* sank.
5   *Swan Lake* was .... by Tchaikovsky.
6   The radio was .... by Marconi.
7   *Macbeth* was .... by Shakespeare.
8   The villages were .... by an earthquake.

11 ▷ **Match.**

Ex.	*The birthday cake*	a	was sent home from school.
1	Our bicycles	b	was broken by a falling tree.
2	My friend	c	*was made by my wife.*
3	The race	d	was won by Stephen.
4	The window	e	were repaired by a shoemaker.
5	My boots	f	was built a very long time ago.
6	This house	g	were repaired by my father.

12 ▷ **Check (✓) the correct sentence.**

Ex. *Were you taken to your hotel on the tour guide?* _____
Were you taken to your hotel by the tour guide? _✓_

1 Was breakfast served in the dining room? _____
Were breakfast served in the dining room? _____

2 Was the towels put in the closet? _____
Were the towels put in the closet? _____

3 Your room it was cleaned by a maid? _____
Was your room cleaned by a maid? _____

4 Were the towels washed in a machine? _____
Was the towels washed in a machine? _____

5 Were the desserts be made at the hotel? _____
Were the desserts made at the hotel? _____

6 Was the meal cooked from your cousin? _____
Was the meal cooked by your cousin? _____

13 ▷ **Find the mistakes and write the sentences correctly.**

Ex. *Students isn't taught algebra in elementary school.*
Students aren't taught algebra in elementary school.
....

1 The game were watched by thousands of people.
....

2 The tourists were taken to the game with bus.
....

3 My ticket were bought by my best friend.
....

4 The players is wearing their blue T-shirts today.
....

5 The game was stop by the coach.
....

6 The grass on the field cut the day before the game.
....

14 ▶ **Answer the questions in your own words.**

Ex.   *Who is the ironing done by in your house?*
      The ironing is done by my husband.

1   Who were you fed by when you were a baby?
....

2   Who was the last CD you listened to made by?
....

3   Who were you first taught English by?
....

4   Who was your house painted by?
....

5   What was the last present you were given?
....

6   Last night who was your dinner made by?
....

Pairwork

Work with a partner. Ask and answer questions using the passive voice.
Talk about the things that were done for you when you were a small child.
For example:

Who made your breakfast?
My breakfast was made by my mother.

➤ Who put you to sleep?   ➤ Who took you out?
➤ Who bought your clothes?   ➤ Who read you stories?
➤ Who bathed you?   ➤ Who taught you to read?

Writing

Imagine you won a competition for yourself and one other person to spend three hours in the world's best department store. You were allowed to take whatever you wanted without paying, as long as you and your partner could carry it. You were taken to the store last night. It had clothes, shoes, food, jewelry and everything else you can imagine. Write about who you chose to go with you, how you were taken to the store (by taxi, by limousine?), who you were served by, what was brought out for you to see and what was taken by you and your partner in the end. Use the passive voice as much as you can.

Last night I was given the chance of a lifetime. My partner and I were taken to ....
....
....
....
....
....
....
....
....
....
....
....

Comparison of Adjectives & Adverbs of Manner

I'LL CARRY IT. I'M STRONGER THAN YOU!

office 31

office 32

Comparatives

We can use the comparative form of an adjective to compare two people, animals or things.
She's older than her brother.
Our car is faster than yours.

We make the comparative form of one-syllable adjectives and most two-syllable adjectives
by adding *-er* to the adjective.
strong ➜ *stronger*

When the adjective ends in *-e*, we add *-r*.
nice ➜ *nicer*

When the adjective has one syllable and ends in vowel–consonant,
we double the final consonant and add *-er*.
hot ➜ *hotter*

When the adjective ends in *-y*, we take off the *-y* and add *-ier*.
easy ➜ *easier*

We use the word *more* with some adjectives that have two syllables
and all adjectives that have three or more syllables.
beautiful ➜ *more beautiful*

Notes

Some two-syllable adjectives (for example,
friendly, handsome, happy, polite, quiet)
can use both forms of the comparative.
polite ➜ *politer / more polite*

We often use the word *than* after the
comparative form.
Rock climbing is more dangerous than golf.

---

1 ▶ Write the comparative form of the adjectives.

Ex. *cold* ....*colder*............

1 long .... 6 busy ....

2 funny .... 7 big ....

3 lazy .... 8 young ....

4 dangerous .... 9 nervous ....

5 polite .... 10 exciting ....

2 ▷ **Complete the sentences with the comparative form of the adjective in parentheses.**

Ex. *This butterfly is* ....*prettier*............... *than the one I saw yesterday. (pretty)*

1 My boss is .... than yours. (nice)

2 This exercise is .... than the last one. (difficult)

3 Our car is .... than the bus. (fast)

4 His life is .... than mine. (easy)

5 Geography is .... than history. (interesting)

6 Our dog is .... than our cat. (old)

7 My daughter's hair is .... than mine. (long)

8 Today is .... than yesterday. (hot)

Superlatives

We can use the superlative form of adjectives to compare people, animals or things in a group of three or more.
She's the tallest girl in the class.
Our house is the oldest in the neighborhood.

We make the superlative form of one-syllable adjectives and most two-syllable adjectives by adding *-est* to the adjective.
strong ➜ *the strongest*

When the adjective ends in *-e*, we add *-st*.
nice ➜ *the nicest*

When the adjective has one syllable and ends in vowel–consonant, we double the final consonant and add *-est*.
hot ➜ *the hottest*

When the adjective ends in *-y*, we take off the *-y* and add *-iest*.
easy ➜ *the easiest*

We use the word *most* with some adjectives that have two syllables and all adjectives that have three or more syllables.
beautiful ➜ *the most beautiful*

Some two-syllable adjectives (for example, *friendly, handsome, happy, polite, quiet*) can use both forms of the superlative.
polite ➜ *politest / most polite*

We use the word *the* before the adjective in its superlative form. We often use a phrase beginning with *in* or *of* to continue the sentence.
What's the hottest desert in the world?
Ann is the tallest of all my friends.

3 ▷ **Write the superlative form of the adjectives.**

Ex. *long* ....*the longest*.............

1 nice ....

2 friendly ....

3 nasty ....

4 hot ....

5 beautiful ....

6 quiet ....

7 careful ....

8 clean ....

4 ▷ **Complete the sentences with the superlative form of the adjective in parentheses.**

Ex. *Who is* ....*the youngest*............ *person in your family? (young)*

1 Linda has .... car of all my friends. (expensive)

2 I have .... desk in my office.

3 Who is .... person in the world? (old)

4 Ed's bedroom is .... room in the house. (messy)

5 I'll carry .... box for you. (large)

6 The living room is .... room in the house. (large)

7 You are .... person I know! (lazy)

8 That was .... movie I've ever seen. (funny)

Irregular Adjectives

Some adjectives have irregular comparative and superlative forms.

good	➜	better	➜	the best
bad	➜	worse	➜	the worst
much/many	➜	more	➜	the most
little	➜	less	➜	the least
far	➜	farther	➜	the farthest

5 ▷ **Complete the sentences with the comparative or superlative form of the adjectives.**

Ex. You have ....*less*............ money than me. (little)

1 I think that was .... movie I've ever seen. (bad)

2 My house is .... from the city than my mother's house. (far)

3 I got .... questions wrong than you did. (many)

4 You're .... friend in the world! (good)

5 This year's office party was .... than last year's. (good)

6 My last job was .... than this one. (bad)

7 Cathy ate .... ice cream than Jessie. (much)

8 Tom does .... work than Mike, but Tim does .... work of all. (little)

6 ▷ **Choose the correct answer.**

Ex. Your dog is .... than ours.

   a noisiest   **ⓑ** noisier   **c** the noisier

1 He's .... man I've ever seen.
   a the more handsome   **b** handsomest   **c** the most handsome

2 Sue's report is .... than Sandra's.
   a good than   **b** better than   **c** best of

3 The weather in Florida is .... the weather in New York.
   a hotter than   **b** more hot   **c** the hottest

4 There are .... people in China than there are in the United States.
   a many   **b** much   **c** more

5 Rick's cell phone is .... I have seen.
   a smallest   **b** smaller than   **c** the smallest

6 .... river in the world is the Nile.
   a Long   **b** The longest   **c** Longer than

7 My dog is always .... than my cat.
   a hungriest   **b** hungry   **c** hungrier

8 She has .... money than her friends.
   a little   **b** much   **c** less

7 ▸ **Find the mistakes and write the sentences correctly.**

Ex. *Our house is cleanest than theirs.*

   Our house is cleaner than theirs.
   ....

1 James is the more intelligent boy in our school.

   ....

2 I'm thin than my sister.

   ....

3 Who has highest score on the test?

   ....

4 This is the bad cake I've ever eaten.

   ....

5 Math is difficult than history.

   ....

6 She is the most tall girl in our class.

   ....

7 My cousin's house is more bigger than my house.

   ....

8 The Gateway Arch is a most famous landmark in Saint Louis.

   ....

Adverbs of Manner

We use adverbs of manner to show the way someone does something. Adverbs of manner answer the question *How?*
(How does she sing?) *She sings beautifully.*
(How does he speak?) *He speaks quickly.*

We form most adverbs by adding *-ly* to the adjective.
quick ➜ *quickly*

When the adjective ends in *-le*, we usually take off the *-e* and add *-y*.
gentle ➜ *gently*

When the adjective ends in *-l*, we add *-ly*.
careful ➜ *carefully*

When the adjective ends in *-y*, we take off the *-y* and add *-ily*.
easy ➜ *easily*
happy ➜ *happily*

8 ▸ **Change these adjectives to adverbs of manner.**

Ex. *nice*   *nicely*

1 slow   ....

2 quick   ....

3 careless ....

4 angry   ....

5 quiet   ....

6 excited   ....

7 rude   ....

8 happy   ....

9 ▶ **Complete the sentences with the adverb form of the adjective in parentheses.**

Ex. *Please don't speak* ....*rudely*........ *to the assistant. (rude)*

1 She rocked the baby .... (gentle)

2 I don't want you to play your music .... (loud)

3 You should drive .... near schools. (slow)

4 He answered all the questions on the TV show .... (easy)

5 My father drives very .... (careful)

6 You shouldn't do your work .... (careless)

7 He walked out of the room and slammed the door .... (angry)

8 The dog is behaving .... (strange)

Irregular Adverbs of Manner

Some adverbs are irregular and do not follow these rules.

good	→	well	late	→	late
fast	→	fast	early	→	early
hard	→	hard	near	→	near
high	→	high			

10 ▶ **Choose the correct answer.**

Ex. *He drives his car very* fastly / (fast)

1 Why did he arrive home *lately / late* last night?

2 I can play the piano very *good / well*.

3 I work *hardest / hard* every day.

4 Look at that kite. It's flying *high / higher* than all the others.

5 I'm glad you got a raise. You worked *hard / hardly*.

6 He ran very *good / well* in the marathon.

Think about it

Mary works hard. Tom hardly works.

Who works harder? Mary, of course.

Hard is an adverb of manner meaning "with great energy, intensely." **Hardly** is an adverb of degree meaning "almost not at all."

11 ▶ **Complete the sentences with the adverbs from the box.**

angrily	fast	happily	politely	quickly	sadly	well

Ex. *The waiter broke all the plates and his boss shouted at him* ....*angrily*............ .

1 The small children played .... while their mothers sat and talked.

2 "I feel terrible. I didn't get the job," he said ....

3 He ran really .... but he didn't win the race.

4 I didn't know you could sing ....

5 The old man was lucky that the ambulance arrived ....

6 I prefer young people who speak ....

12 ▶ **Find the mistakes and write the sentences correctly.**

Ex. *He spoke quiet, so I didn't hear him.*
     He spoke quietly, so I didn't hear him.

1 Harry has a fast sports car, but he drives it careful.

   ....

2 I can only understand you if you speak slowest.

   ....

3 He sings badly but he plays the guitar good.

   ....

4 We can easy win the game.

   ....

5 If you're sitting comfortable, I'll tell you a story.

   ....

13 ▶ **Complete the second sentence so that it has a similar meaning to the first sentence.**

Ex. *Susan is a beautiful dancer.*

   Susan .... *dances beautifully.* ....

1 Those boys are good football players.

   Those boys play ....

2 Jim is careless when he washes the dishes.

   Jim washes ....

3 Mandy is always polite when she speaks to her parents.

   Mandy always speaks ....

4 Our cat is happy when she plays with her toys.

   Our cat plays ....

5 Frank always makes noise when he eats soup.

   Frank always eats ....

6 Jessie is a fast driver when he's late.

   Jessie drives ....

14 ▶ **Answer the questions in your own words.**

Ex. *What do you do badly?*
     I sing badly.

     Who is the oldest in your family?
     My grandfather is the oldest in my family.

1 What do you do well?

   ....

   ....

2 What does your friend do well?

   ....

   ....

3 Who is the funniest person you know?

   ....

   ....

4 What do you do slowly?

   ....

   ....

5 What can you do quickly?

   ....

   ....

Pairwork

Work with a partner. Take turns. Ask and answer about how your partner does the things below. Then ask three questions of your own. For example:
How do you sing? Badly!
How do you walk to work? Slowly.

➤ sing
➤ draw
➤ play basketball
➤ eat your food

➤ ride a bicycle
➤ talk to your classmates
➤ behave when you're out

Writing

Write a short essay about your family or friends. Write as much as you can about each person. Use comparatives and superlatives to compare them.

....
....
....
....
....
....
....
....
....
....
....
....
....
....

Present Perfect Continuous

WHO HAS BEEN USING MY COMPUTER AGAIN?

office 48

Present Perfect Continuous

Affirmative	Negative	Question
I have (I've) been working	I have not (haven't) been working	Have I been working?
you have (you've) been working	you have not (haven't) been working	Have you been working?
he has (he's) been working	he has not (hasn't) been working	Has he been working?
she has (she's) been working	she has not (hasn't) been working	Has she been working?
it has (it's) been working	it has not (hasn't) been working	Has it been working?
we have (we've) been working	we have not (haven't) been working	Have we been working?
you have (you've) been working	you have not (haven't) been working	Have you been working?
they have (they've) been working	they have not (haven't) been working	Have they been working?

Short Answers

Yes, I/you have.	No, I/you haven't
Yes, he/she/it has.	No, he/she/it hasn't.
Yes, we/you/they have.	No, we/you/they haven't.

We use the Present Perfect Continuous to talk about:

➤ something that started in the past and that has been repeated or continued until now.
How long have you been living here?
She's been working all day.

➤ something that happened repeatedly or continuously in the past, but we can still see the result now.
They have been running. (They are tired and out of breath.)
She's been painting the house. (Her hands and clothes are covered in paint.)

---

1 ► **Complete the sentences with the Present Perfect Continuous.**

Ex. *Jim* .....*has been painting*....... *the living room since 8 o'clock. (paint)*

1   He .... to classical music since he was a teenager. (listen)

2   I .... e-mails all morning. (write)

3   My husband .... dinner for an hour now. (cook)

4   The children .... television all morning. (watch)

5   It .... for the last ten days. (rain)

6   We .... for hours! (wait)

Thinkabout**it**

With the Present Perfect Continuous, we always use **have/has been** and the main verb + **-ing**.

2 ▶ **Make the sentences negative.**

Ex. *We've been studying English since we were two years old.*
   We haven't been studying English since we were two years old.

1   I've been working here since last June.

   ....

2   The dog has been barking all night.

   ....

3   I have been waiting for a long time.

   ....

4   He has been feeling very well since this morning.

   ....

5   They've been discussing the problem for weeks.

   ....

6   The baby has been crying for a few minutes.

   ....

3 ▶ **Write questions in the Present Perfect Continuous.**

Ex. *you / clean / the bathroom / ?*
   Have you been cleaning the bathroom?

1   he / lie / in bed / since this morning / ?   4   she / make / cakes / all day / ?
   ....

2   they / dance / all night / ?   5   it / snow / since last night / ?
   ....

3   you / study / all morning / ?   6   he / walk / in the park / ?
   ....

Time Expressions

We can use the words *for* and *since* with the Present Perfect Continuous.

for + a period of time
(e.g., *a week, three days*)
I've been living here for two years.

since + a point in time (e.g., *last month, when I was young*)
He's been driving since 10 o'clock this morning.

4 ▶ **Complete the sentences with for or since.**

Ex. *They've been watching television ......since...... 9 o'clock this morning.*

1   I've been working in the bank .... 1997.

2   He's been building the house .... three weeks.

3   I've been listening to the radio .... the last two hours.

4   We've been living in this house .... we built it.

5   Joe's been fixing his bike .... 11 o'clock this morning.

6   She's been doing her homework .... hours!

7   The cat has been sleeping on the sofa .... hours.

8   I've been feeling old .... my last birthday.

5 Check (✓) the correct sentence.

Ex. *The sun's been shining since hours.* _____
The sun's been shining for hours. __✓__

1 Jake's been painting pictures since he was thirteen. _____
Jake's been painting pictures for he was thirteen. _____

2 Alan's been cleaning the kitchen for two hours. _____
Alan's been cleaning the kitchen since two hours. _____

3 Greg and June have been dance for hours. _____
Greg and June have been dancing for hours. _____

4 We've been travel all night. _____
We've been traveling all night. _____

5 He's been climbing mountains since he was a young boy. _____
He's be climbing mountains since he was a young boy. _____

6 We have been living in Atlanta for 1999. _____
We have been living in Atlanta since 1999. _____

6 Match.

Ex. *There are dirty dishes in the kitchen.*
1 There is a wet towel and sand on the floor.
2 There are stamps and envelopes on the desk.
3 There is a wet umbrella in the hall.
4 There is flour and sugar on the kitchen floor.
5 There are paint cans and brushes on the table.
6 There are CDs on the living room floor.

a Dan has been swimming.
b It's been raining.
c I've been painting my room.
d We've been listening to music.
e Jenny has been writing letters.
f The children have been making a cake.
g *Diane's been making dinner.*

7 Choose the correct answer.

Ex. *They haven't .... speaking to each other for days.*
a to   **(b)** been   **c** be

1 Tim has been .... for a new job since last year.
a looking   **b** look   **c** looked

2 Scientists have been studying the planet Mars ....
many years.
a since   **b** after   **c** for

3 Mrs. Johnson .... been teaching English since
she was 25.
a has   **b** have   **c** was

4 .... they been studying hard all morning?
a Are   **b** Have   **c** Did

5 The comedian has been telling jokes .... evening.
a for   **b** since   **c** all

6 Tom has been working on his car .... he woke up
this morning.
a for   **b** after   **c** since

8 Write the words in the correct order.

Ex. *for / has / she / exercising / hours / been / two*
She has been exercising for two hours.

1 since / have / hard / been / breakfast / working / they / ?
....
....

2 this / years / has / she / for / doing / been / job
....
....

3 was / been / I / sixteen / perfume / using / have / this /
since / I
....
....

4 been / for / he / reading / book / months / has / six / that
....
....

5 not / long / been / we / living / have / here / for
....
....

9 ▶ **Answer the questions in your own words.**

Ex. *How long have you been living in your house?*
I have been living in my house since I was born.
....

1   How long have you been learning English?
....

2   How long have you been working?
....

3   What have you been doing today?
....

4   What have you been studying in English this week?
....

5   How long have you been living in this area?

....

Pairwork

Work with a partner. Talk about things you have been doing for a long time and things you have been doing for a short time. For example:

I have been living here for eight years.
I have been working in the library for two weeks.

Writing

Write an e-mail to a friend about what you have been doing this month. Use the Present Perfect Continuous where possible.

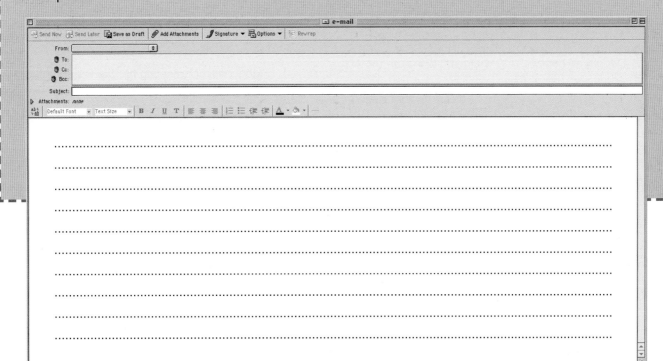

Review 5 (Units 17-20)

1 ▶ Complete the sentences using gerunds.

Ex. ....*Driving*......... a car can be dangerous. (drive)

1 My brothers both hate .... (swim)

2 Dad goes .... every morning. (jog)

3 Her hobbies include .... and karate. (cook)

4 My mother spends a lot of time .... (sew)

5 .... too much tea or coffee is bad for you. (drink)

6 .... a horse is good exercise. (ride)

7 She's very good at different types of .... (dance)

8 .... fruits and vegetables is good for your health. (eat)

3 ▶ Choose the correct answer.

Ex. *He has stopped .... cakes and sweets.*
    a *to eat*   **b** *eat*   ⓒ *eating*

1 We were surprised .... that our neighbor was a famous actor.
   a to find out   **b** finding out   **c** found out

2 I'm not interested in .... about history.
   a to learn   **b** learn   **c** learning

3 I would be happy .... help you with your project.
   a in   **b** to   **c** for

4 She's excited about .... how to water ski.
   a to learn   **b** learning   **c** learns

5 I want .... to New Zealand next year.
   a to go   **b** going   **c** to be gone

6 The boss won't allow her .... the day off.
   a taking   **b** to take   **c** take

7 I've decided .... art in college.
   a to study   **b** studying   **c** for to study

8 We can't stand .... reports.
   a to write   **b** to writing   **c** writing

2 ▶ Complete the sentences with the gerund form of the words from the box.

act	check	eat	help	join
laugh	listen	wait	watch	

Ex. *She can't help ......*laughing*..... when she sees him.*

1 My friends love .... Chinese food.

2 Are you interested in .... an environmental group?

3 I can't stand .... in long lines.

4 I really miss .... movies with my parents now that I have my own apartment.

5 My sister is very good at .... She is in a theater group.

6 She dislikes .... to loud rock music.

7 They don't mind .... us clean up after the party.

8 I never leave home without .... the weather forecast.

4 ▶ Find the extra word in each sentence and write it on the dotted line.

Ex. *I love to taking a hot shower every morning.*
    ....*to*............

1 Meg loves for meeting her friends at night.
   ....

2 Jack hates being it the only person at home at night. ....

3 Do you like to going out to eat?
   ....

4 I'm tired of it hearing about your problems every day! ....

5 We love are watching old movies on TV.
   ....

6 She promised to be give me the money back soon. ....

5 ▶ **Complete the sentences with is or are.**

Ex. *Race cars ......are...... driven by expert drivers.*

1 Lots of tea .... grown in China.

2 Most cars .... made in large factories.

3 My favorite perfume .... sold in only two shops in this town.

4 Soccer and basketball .... played all over the world.

5 Some rare animals .... kept in zoos.

6 My shoes .... made in Italy.

7 The World Cup .... watched by millions of people every four years.

8 These desks .... made of wood.

6 ▶ **Complete the sentences with was or were.**

Ex. *Television ......was...... invented by John Logie Baird.*

1 The woman .... given a huge bunch of flowers.

2 Those flowers .... picked from my garden.

3 The picture *The Sunflowers* .... painted by Van Gogh.

4 Mount Everest .... climbed by Sir Edmund Hillary.

5 The championship game .... seen by millions of people.

6 A new star .... discovered by astronomers last year.

7 The Pyramids .... built by the ancient Egyptians.

8 The role of Hamlet .... played by a famous actor.

7 ▶ **Change the sentences from active to passive.**

Ex. *Birds build nests.*
    Nests are built by birds.
....

1 Did a friend of yours design this bracelet?
....

2 Someone makes these T-shirts for our school.
....

3 Tim didn't fix the bicycle.
....

4 The storm caused the damage.
....

5 Who told Steve?
....

6 William Shakespeare wrote *Hamlet*.
....

7 Someone stole my bicycle.
....

8 Did somebody find a wallet in the cafeteria?
....

Review 5

8 ▸ Complete the sentences with the comparative form of the word in parentheses.

Ex. *I am ....younger.......... than you. (young)*

1   He works .... than anybody I know. (hard)

2   She is .... cat I have ever seen! (beautiful)

3   Is skiing .... than driving? (dangerous)

4   Fruit is .... for you than chocolate. (good)

5   Is your wife .... than your daughter? (tall)

6   The streets in small towns are .... than in big cities. (clean)

7   My headache is .... than it was an hour ago. (bad)

8   I think you're .... than me! (intelligent)

9 ▸ Complete the sentences with the superlative form of the adjectives.

Ex. *That's the ....biggest.......... dog I've ever seen. (big)*

1   My best friend is .... person in the world! (nice)

2   Are elephants .... animals in the world? (strong)

3   What's .... movie you've ever watched? (bad)

4   She's .... baby I've ever seen. (happy)

5   Which dinosaur was ....? (large)

6   They make .... pizza at that restaurant. (good)

7   I'm sitting on .... chair in the house. (comfortable)

8   What's .... thing you've ever done? (dangerous)

10 ▸ Choose the correct answer.

Ex. *My brother acts .... than my sister.*
   ⓐ *sillier*   **b** *silly*   **c** *silliest*

1   She has longer hair .... me.
   a of   **b** than   **c** as

2   That's .... most beautiful park in the city.
   a the   **b** than   **c** a

3   What could be .... enjoyable than lying on the beach?
   a most   **b** more   **c** as

4   What is the .... expensive thing in the store?
   a most   **b** more   **c** little

5   Who's got the .... work to do?
   a less   **b** little   **c** least

6   Which restaurant has the .... food in town?
   a best   **b** good   **c** bad

11 ▸ Complete the sentences with adverbs.

Ex. *We waited ....patiently.......... for the doctor to arrive. (patient)*

1   The boy ran .... down the road. (quick)

2   My head hurts. Don't play your drums so ....! (loud)

3   They laughed .... at many of my jokes. (happy)

4   She counted the money .... (careful)

5   You must speak .... in the library. (quiet)

6   Why are you driving so ....? (fast)

7   You shouldn't work so .... all the time. (hard)

8   Why is he shouting so ....? (angry)

12 ▶ **Complete the sentences with the Present Perfect Continuous.**

Ex. *She* .... *has been living* .... *in that house since 1990. (live)*

1 The birds .... their chicks. (feed)
2 The rain .... for hours. (fall)
3 My brother .... for a new home. (look)
4 .... the rabbit .... holes? (dig)
5 The foxes .... chickens. (not steal)
6 The owls .... all night. (fly)
7 .... the bears .... all winter? (sleep)
8 The dogs .... since this morning. (bark)

13 ▶ **Choose the correct answer.**

Ex. *He* .... *learning to drive for six months.*
   (a) *has been*   **b** *is*   **c** *was being*

1 The computer has not .... working for three days.
   a be   **b** been   **c** being

2 Why have you been .... at everybody today?
   a shouting   **b** shouted   **c** shouts

3 .... he been waiting long?
   a Have   **b** Did   **c** Has

4 I've .... learning to swim this summer.
   a been   **b** being   **c** be

5 He's been waiting for you .... this afternoon.
   a for   **b** at   **c** since

6 Neil's been reading the same book for ....
   a weeks   **b** 9 o'clock   **c** all evening

7 I've been sleeping .... morning.
   a for   **b** since   **c** all

8 She's been playing the drums .... years.
   a since   **b** for   **c** in

14 ▶ **Find the extra word in each sentence and write it on the dotted line.**

Ex. *Where have they the children been playing?* .... *they* ....

1 How long for have you been living alone? ....
2 She has been talking on the phone for thirty minutes ago. ....
3 The baby it has been crying all day. ....
4 What has Dan been doing since at school all day? ....
5 Russell's has been looking for his keys for hours. ....
6 We haven't have been waiting for very long. ....
7 People have and been using computers for many years. ....
8 How long since has it been raining? ....

Irregular Verbs

Infinitive	Simple Past	Past Participle	Infinitive	Simple Past	Past Participle
be	was/were	been	lead	led	led
become	became	become	leave	left	left
begin	began	begun	lend	lent	lent
blow	blew	blown	lose	lost	lost
break	broke	broken	make	made	made
bring	brought	brought	meet	met	met
build	built	built	pay	paid	paid
buy	bought	bought	put	put	put
catch	caught	caught	read	read	read
choose	chose	chosen	ride	rode	ridden
come	came	come	ring	rang	rung
cut	cut	cut	run	ran	run
do	did	done	say	said	said
draw	drew	drawn	see	saw	seen
drink	drank	drunk	sell	sold	sold
drive	drove	driven	shine	shone	shone
eat	ate	eaten	show	showed	shown
fall	fell	fallen	sing	sang	sung
feed	fed	fed	sit	sat	sat
feel	felt	felt	sleep	slept	slept
find	found	found	speak	spoke	spoken
fly	flew	flown	spend	spent	spent
forget	forgot	forgotten	stand	stood	stood
get	got	gotten/got	swim	swam	swum
give	gave	given	take	took	taken
go	went	gone	teach	taught	taught
grow	grew	grown	tell	told	told
have	had	had	think	thought	thought
hear	heard	heard	understand	understood	understood
hit	hit	hit	wake	woke	woken
hurt	hurt	hurt	wear	wore	worn
keep	kept	kept	win	won	won
know	knew	known	write	wrote	written

Notes

Notes

Notes